The Happiness Equation

Bridget Grenville-Cleave and Ilona Boniwell, Ph.D.
with Tina B. Tessina, Ph.D.

Contents

Introduction

The founding fathers of our country saw the "pursuit of happiness" as an inalienable right—so important that they embedded it in the DNA of the United States of America by writing it into the Preamble to the Constitution. It was a profoundly new idea at the time. With it, they set wheels in motion that have been turning ever since.

In my private counseling practice, clients often tell me, "I want to be happy!" We then set about making it a reality. *The Happiness Equation* can help you look at your own behavior, thoughts, and feelings objectively and change the things that are negatively affecting your happiness. With each entry labeled as a positive or negative factor, you can clearly see where you stand. But more important than rating yourself is to take each item to heart and put it into practice.

There is a genetic component that scientists say is responsible for many people feeling unhappy or depressed. But don't let that discourage you, because it's obvious as I work with people that genetic makeup is not the only factor that affects mood. Your habits, your relationships, your environment, and especially what you think about them have a huge impact. As a psychotherapist, I know that those things determine more about how happy you are than your genes do, because I've watched so many people learn how happiness works.

You can improve every area of your happiness: your relationship with yourself and with others, your work life, your home life, and even your health. While you're at it, take a little time to congratulate yourself on your personal pursuit of happiness, because Celebration + Appreciation = Motivation. The more you understand that increasing your happiness is working, the more motivated you will be, and the happier you can become. As you discover the factors in this book that are most effective for you, make a little reminder note about the best ones. Keep it handy, so if your happiness level starts to slide, you can bring it back up to where you want it. And have a happy life!

Tina B. Tessina, Ph.D., psychotherapist and author of *Money, Sex, and Kids: Stop Fighting About the Three Things That Can Ruin Your Marriage*

How to use this book

The Happiness Equation presents the 100 factors which most influence human well-being and happiness, either positively or negatively. The information in this book is based on the latest scientific studies and academic research, explaining which aspects of life circumstances, day-to-day activities, and emotions most affect our level of happiness. Of course, people are individuals with their own wants and needs: what works for me isn't necessarily the same for you. Science shows us, however, that there are some aspects of happiness which are pretty widespread across the globe, so most of the factors in this book will be relevant to your own life. Plus or minus points have been allocated to each factor to give you some idea of their relative importance.

Some factors that are known to affect your happiness are fixed (like your genes and personality) and some can be changed (like your life circumstances and outlook on life). Many positive psychologists agree that happiness is made up as follows:

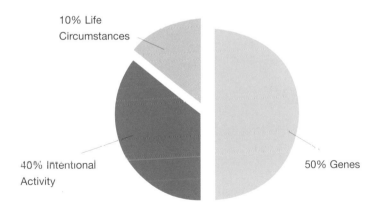

10% Life
Circumstances

40% Intentional
Activity

50% Genes

So before you dive into the book, start by considering your genetic make-up. Studies have been carried out on sets of identical and non-identical twins to establish the link between our happiness levels and our genes.The results allow us to conclude that genes account for about 50 percent of the difference between our individual level of happiness and everyone else's. So whether or not you have "happy genes" is the most dominant factor that affects your happiness. As yet there is no medical test which can accurately determine your happiness "set-point," so make an educated guess or ask your parents and grandparents about their happiness. Just make sure they give you an honest answer! If you've been dealt a good hand you can allocate yourself 50 points straight away. Or if you think you weren't, allocate fewer. Once you've decided on your genetic baseline, you can add or subtract points depending on whether or not the factors in the book relate to you and your lifestyle.

Just because your happiness baseline is for the most part genetically determined does not mean that you cannot become happier. What the Happiness Pie shows us is that 40 percent of your happiness is within your control, i.e. there are a whole range of activities you can do to increase (or decrease) your happiness, some of which are outlined in this book. The remaining 10 percent of the Pie is influenced by life circumstances, such as age, gender, social class and the community you live in. These factors are outlined in Part 1, but they make only a small difference to your level of happiness, and probably not as much as you might think. Parts 2 to 5 present some of the daily activities and emotions which influence the remaining 40 percent of your happiness. These are the areas of your life where you can really make a conscious effort to improve your happiness, so try some of the positive activities, or at least try to avoid the negative ones.

Research suggests that the majority of people are quite happy, which would equate to around 68 points. If you can collect more than that, you're doing well! If you score under 64 points, try taking up some of the positive activites in Parts 2 to 5 to give your happiness a boost. Once you've finished adding and subtracting your way through the book, look here to see how you measure up:

POINTS

Over 91:	☺☺☺☺	On cloud 9!
Between 76-90:	☺☺☺	Very happy.
Between 65-75:	☺☺	Pretty cheerful.
Under 64:	☺	Less happy than average.

A word of caution: everyone is an individual and it is impossible in to predict with 100 percent certainty how happy or not you'll be if you participate in or refrain from the various activities. So please don't take the results too seriously. This book should be seen as a way of getting you to think about what you can do differently to boost your happiness. And if you have real concerns about either your mental or physical well-being, consult your doctor, therapist, or a counselor immediately.

Often when we think about our happiness (or more usually, our unhappiness) we have a tendency to think in terms of "If Only." Such as, if only I were younger, I'd be happy. Or if only I were thinner, or better looking, or richer. But the factor which most influences your level of well-being is your genes, which you cannot change, although maybe one day in the future scientific advancements may allow this!

After your genes, research reveals that your life circumstances make a pretty small difference to your happiness. So even though you may get a new job, buy a new car, emigrate to a sunnier country or even, as improbable as this may sound, win the lottery, these events are highly unlikely to show up as more than a temporary blip on your happiness baseline. Of course there are other reasons to pursue a career, or move to a new house or country, so no one is suggesting that you shouldn't do these things if they're right for you. What is important is that you manage your expectations. And don't be surprised if, a few months after you've started your new job or moved, you find that the change didn't increase your happiness as much as you thought it would.

PART ONE

Life Circumstances

Aging

☺ 0.5 POINTS

What would you say is the happiest time of your life? Perhaps childhood, when all you do is play, play, play. Maybe early adulthood, when you've left home and you're embarking on an exciting career. Not many people would mention adolescence (puberty), mid-life (crisis!) or old age (fading health and faculties).

The interesting thing is that we're remarkably bad at remembering accurately how happy we were in the past and predicting how happy we'll be in the future. For example, older people believe 30-year-olds are much happier than they themselves were at age 30. We also expect to be happier when we're in a romantic relationship, when we're promoted, or when we lose weight. As it happens, these events may boost our happiness level temporarily, but then the effect wears off and it returns pretty quickly to what it was before.

The same thing happens with negative events. Many of us think that if we became seriously ill, for example, we'd be substantially less happy, but in fact most people adjust to their circumstances over time and are only marginally less happy, if at all. This inability to predict our happiness accurately might be one of the reasons why we're afraid of getting older—we expect to be less happy.

In fact, happiness has more to do with the process of aging. Typically, happiness levels start high, then decline, reaching a low point around the mid-40s, and then increase again. So why don't we become more unhappy as we age, as we face poorer health, probable widowhood, and dwindling finances? One answer may be that as we mature, we reprioritize, redirecting our energies away from things we can't do to toward things we can, focusing on more meaningful social and emotional goals rather than on material acquisition. So don't worry that you'll be a grumpy senior citizen; in all likelihood you'll be happier than you were in your 40s.

Gender

0.5 POINTS ☺

In recent years, in the workplace at least, we've been encouraged to acknowledge and celebrate the differences between the sexes, recognizing that both have unique strengths (and weaknesses). When it comes to happiness, however, it seems that men and women are roughly equally happy in nearly every country, suggesting that gender per se has little effect on happiness.

There is evidence that women's overall well-being is more influenced by events that happened in the past, while men's is more influenced by recent events. Not only that but women, on the whole, show more intense positive emotion than men, as well as more negative emotion, typically depression. Put another way, women are both happier and unhappier than men! Although there's no scientific evidence that this greater emotional intensity interferes with job performance or any other responsibilities or capabilities, this might explain why women are frequently labeled as the "more sensitive" sex. In today's high stress world, more emotional stability is perceived to give men a slight advantage.

3

Money, money, money...

☺ **0.5 POINTS**

The results from studies in which people have been asked to rate their happiness on a scale of 1 to 10, show that the average level of happiness across the globe is currently about 6.75 out of 10, so it's quite likely that you're already pretty happy in life. But it's money that makes the world go round, if the popular saying and the hit musical *Cabaret* are to be believed, so does having more money actually make you happier?

Comparison of wealth and happiness by country

Country	GDP per capita ($)	% satisfied with life
USA	46,000	65
Canada	38,200	71
GB	35,300	59
Germany	34,400	48
France	33,800	57
Poland	16,200	39
Peru	7,600	41
India	2,700	41
Kenya	1,600	16
Uganda	1,100	7

When we're comparing different countries, it's easy to see that the level of happiness rises as wealth increases. Bear in mind that other factors may contribute to the strength of this wealth-happiness link, though. Richer industrially developed countries also tend to be more democratic than poorer less developed ones, for example.

Would a higher income make you as an individual happier? "Yes of course!" you say without hesitation—"just think of all those things you could do with the extra money." Wealthier people are a little happier than the rest of us, it turns out, but not as much as you might think.

As it happens, the average annual income in developed countries has been growing steadily since the end of World War II, but happiness levels have not risen at the same rate. In the US for example, between 1970 and 1990 average incomes rose by 300 percent in real terms, but average well-being hasn't risen correspondingly.

The reason for this seems to be that people care more about their relative income than they do about their absolute income; in one study, Harvard students actually preferred to earn half as much, as long as they were still better off than everyone else! So, if everyone else is also getting richer, your happiness won't increase as much.

But don't let this stop you asking for that pay rise you've been dreaming of for months; just remember that the increase in happiness you feel when you get it might not be as much as you'd expect, and it might not last as long either. For more information on how your "happiness set-point" works, see entry 19.

4

Feeling healthy

☺ **2 POINTS**

Ever since Hippocrates, we have suspected a link between physical and psychological health, such that negative emotional experiences make us more vulnerable to falling ill, whereas positive ones can fortify us. So you won't be surprised to know that the immune systems of happy people are more effective than those of people who are not. Positive emotions also increase pain tolerance and can even protect us against death from alcohol-related liver disease and heart disease, even after adjusting for factors such as age, gender, exercise, alcohol consumption, and smoking.

But does good physical health actually make you happier? In fact your physical health (or ill-health) makes very little difference to happiness, unless you happen to be severely disabled. What matters more is whether or not you think you're healthy! And what you think about your health is influenced more by your personality (see entry 9) and coping strategies than by your objective health. We probably all know someone who complains endlessly about this or that ailment when actually there's nothing physically wrong with them. In contrast, we may have relatives, friends or neighbors who are clearly under the weather, but who say they feel quite well.

So perceptions of health are more important to happiness than actual health. If you have the misfortune to be ill, find ways to think differently about your situation, such as reframing important life goals or comparing yourself to others who are worse off.

5

Unhealthy foods
2 POINTS ☹

What you eat can have a negative effect on both your physical and psychological health. Eating too many saturated fats and trans fatty acids increases the risk of heart disease, obesity, and type 2 diabetes, while evidence is growing that a diet lacking essential vitamins, minerals, and Omega-3s can lead to depression, anxiety, poor concentration, mood swings, and fatigue as well as increased aggression. In one study, vitamins and other vital nutrients were added to the diets of young offenders at a maximum security institution. Researchers found that those prisoners who received the supplements committed 25 percent fewer offences than those who had been given a placebo. In addition serious offences such as violence were reduced by 40 percent.

Foods to avoid

- Processed foods such as bread and ready meals. Some contain added ingredients to make them more appetizing, but they aren't good for you.

- Saturated fats found in dairy products as well as palm oil and coconut oil.

- Alcohol—most adults can drink alcohol in moderation without any problem, but it easily decreases your self-control and impairs your judgement, making risky behavior much more attractive.

- Refined foods such as white sugar, rice, and flour, lack essential nutrients.

- Caffeine stimulates the central nervous system and boosts energy levels, making you feel more alert, but you can develop a tolerance to it quickly, so you need to drink more to get the same effect.

Nutrition

☺ # 2 POINTS

A balanced diet with the right combination of vitamins and minerals is one of the most important contributors to physical health, yet rarely do we discuss its role in happiness and well-being. A diet which draws on all five food groups (starchy carbohydrates; fruit and vegetables; milk and dairy; meat and fish; fat and sugar) will provide the essential vitamins and minerals needed to keep you fit, healthy, and happy.

Vitamins and minerals to boost your mood

- Folic Acid (from broccoli, asparagus, and peas). Folic acid deficiency causes fatigue, confusion, and irritability.

- Vitamin B12 (from meat, salmon, milk, eggs, and yeast extract). Severe vitamin B12 deficiency results in loss of memory, mental dysfunction, and depression.

- Vitamin C (found in peppers, broccoli, oranges, and kiwi fruit). In studies, high-dose vitamin C supplements have been shown to reduce depression.

- Selenium (from brazil nuts, bread, fish, meat, and eggs). In studies, individuals given daily selenium supplements for five

or six weeks showed improved mood scores against those given a placebo.

- Iron (from liver, dried fruit, whole grains, and dark green leafy vegetables). Deficiency leads to fatigue, irritability, apathy, and inability to concentrate.

- Zinc (from meat, shellfish, dairy foods, and cereal products). Depression is a common symptom of zinc deficiency.

- Omega-3 from fatty fish, organic free-range eggs, nuts and seeds, and brown rice. Deficiency is thought to be responsible for increased incidences of depression and anxiety.

7

Beauty

0.5 POINTS ☺

It's only relatively recently that researchers have started to investigate the benefits of beauty from a scientific perspective. For instance, did you know that physically attractive people are considered to be warmer, stronger, and more poised? Good-looking job candidates are more likely to get the job? Attractive criminals are more likely to receive lower prison sentences than unattractive ones? The list goes on. So whether we like it or not, physical attractiveness is a very powerful resource.

Clearly many people put a high value on appearance. According to the American Society of Aesthetic Plastic Surgery nearly 11.5 million operations were carried out in 2006. Of those operations, 92 percent were on women. However, it's not just women; according to Euromonitor International, in 2007 the global men's grooming market was worth almost $22 billion.

But for all that, does your appearance actually make you happier? There is recent research to suggest that Botox can be used to treat depression, by removing the participants' ability to frown. Most people would agree that taking care of your appearance provides an important boost to your self-respect, even though spending thousands of dollars on permanent plastic surgery may only make you feel better in the short run. Clearly there are acknowledged benefits to being more beautiful, and indirectly these may result in your feeling better. It's interesting, however, that happy people tend to believe they're more beautiful, even if other people think they look pretty average. So if you want to be more beautiful, get happy first.

Mental well-being

☺

1 POINT

Imagine a scale measuring mental well-being from -10 to +10. "Traditional" clinical psychology is concerned with helping people who are in the 0 to -10 range, i.e. those who have a mental illness according to the Diagnostic and Statistical Manual of Mental Disorders. Positive psychologists, on the other hand, are more concerned with optimal human functioning, studying those people who are in the 0 to +10 range. Many academics don't make this distinction, but it is an important one.

Research has shown that psychological well-being is not merely the absence of negative emotions; it requires the occurrence of positive emotions, too. Thus if you have the misfortune to suffer from a mental illness, removing or "curing" it (the aim of traditional psychology) does not necessarily mean that you will then flourish and thrive. But some positive psychology interventions—for example, writing a gratitude diary—have been shown in empirical studies to improve psychological well-being; that is, they can actually increase one's level of happiness.

How to improve your mental well-being

- Start every day with meditation.

- Physical exercise—take half an hour of exercise three times a week.

- Write a gratitude diary.

- Keep a house plant.

- Have a good laugh at least once a day.

- Smile at and/or say hello to a stranger at least once a day.

- Do a good deed for someone every day—it doesn't have to be elaborate.

- Lose yourself in a favorite activity, whether it's fly-fishing, stamp-collecting, or learning a foreign language.

Extrovert

1 POINT ☺

The cult of personality appears to be growing ever stronger in this media-rich age, bolstered by 24-hour news, sound-bites, the internet, and "reality TV" shows such as Big Brother. These days there are numerous ways for people to become famous personalities, some deliberately manufactured like the Spice Girls, and others unintentional, like the Australian conservationist and one-time crocodile hunter, the late Steve Irwin.

Personality is something that fascinates everyone—we all have one and it's pretty unique, even if we're not media stars because of it! But do your personality traits dictate how happy you are? Well, according to positive psychologists, not only is personality one of the strongest predictors of subjective well-being, but two specific traits, extroversion (e.g., how talkative, energetic, and assertive you are) and neuroticism (e.g., how tense, moody, and anxious you are), can predict how happy you will be in 10 years time. So if you're high on the extroversion dimension and low on the neuroticism dimension, you're also likely to be pretty happy, too.

If personality traits are that strongly related to one's predisposition towards happiness, there are at least two important implications. Firstly, this helps explain why, once basic needs have been met, people don't get that much happier as they get richer. Secondly, insofar as personality is malleable during early years, parents, guardians, nursery schools, and teachers can help to develop their children's propensity for happiness in later life.

10

Social class

☺ **0.5 POINTS**

The notion of social class exists in many cultures and societies, but the phenomenon isn't universal; there are some cultures, such as hunter-gatherer or nomadic tribes, which are completely non-hierarchical. Generally speaking, in those nation states that have a class system, people from higher social classes tend also to have higher levels of education, higher occupational status, and higher income, therefore it's easy to imagine that they must also be more happy.

In one analysis of 286 empirical studies involving over 150,000 participants across the globe, psychologists Pinquart and Sörensen have shown that higher social class is indeed linked to three measures of well-being, that is, life satisfaction, self-esteem, and happiness.

That may not come as a surprise, but the reason why people of a higher social class enjoy their lives more isn't actually because they earn more money, since this happens even when the effects of income are taken into account. This indicates that there must be other factors at work apart from money.

Psychologists like Daniel Nettle have thought that, rather than money, it's the amount of personal control you have that contributes to well-being, life satisfaction, and health. In one study of over 10,000 British civil servants, for example, researchers discovered that low job control in the work environment contributes to the development of coronary heart disease.

So you're likely to be happier and healthier the more you feel that you can direct the course of your life and manage your health, work, family, and relationships successfully. If it's autonomy, rather than money, which brings happiness, maybe we should encourage children to develop a strong sense of personal control, rather than find a career that will simply make them rich.

Sunshine

0.5 POINTS ☺

Don't you feel so much better when the sun shines? You're more cheerful, more optimistic, more able to deal with life's little problems, and you notice that other people are more helpful and smile more, too. Sunshine has well-known health benefits: the human body uses sunlight to create vitamin D, which protects against many aging-related diseases, such as heart disease, cancer, and rheumatoid arthritis. Plus, it's long been established that sunshine (specifically bright light, rather than warmth) improves mood, by raising the level of serotonin produced by the brain. This helps to explain why light therapy typically has an antidepressant effect on those suffering from seasonal affective disorder (SAD).

According to the Association of American Residents Overseas, there are 6.6 million Americans living outside America—the top 10 countries include Mexico, Israel, and Italy. As for Britons, UK National Statistics show that Australia, France, Spain, and the US are popular emigration destinations. No doubt for many of these people, particularly those retiring, the prospect of a sunny, warm climate was an important factor in their decision-making, so it seems that many people think that living in a sunnier climate will make them happier.

While sunshine can boost how you feel, do keep in mind that over time you will become acclimatized and return to your "normal" happiness baseline (see pages 7–9). Luckily, the same applies to unfavorable weather conditions, and bad weather won't make you miserable for life. So even if sunshine cannot permanently make you happier, it can certainly give you a temporary lift.

12

Community spirit

☺ **0.5 POINTS**

Social relationships are fundamental to human evolution; we wouldn't have survived as a species without the ability to live and work in groups, giving each other support in times of need and sharing in times of plenty. Because of this, the community you live in plays a vital role in your happiness.

The quality of a community tends to be measured in terms of its cohesiveness. This in turn can be defined as a combination of similar factors such as trust, reciprocity, mutual help, and volunteering—although as you might imagine, quantifying cohesiveness can be more problematic! The World Values Survey can be used to provide much-needed insights into the quality of country level communities across the globe, since it includes questions about trust—such as, "Generally speaking, would you say that most people can be trusted or that you need to be very careful in dealing with people?"—as well as asking about the volunteer work that respondents do.

The results show that the proportion of the population who say people can be trusted ranges from 7 percent in Turkey to about 66 percent in Denmark; this is given as one of the reasons why Denmark frequently comes out top or near top in well-being surveys. It is also interesting that in the majority of European countries, the level of trust in society has increased dramatically between 1981 and 1999; the main exception to this is the UK, where the proportion of the population who agree that people can be trusted has fallen from 42.5 percent in 1981 to 28.5 percent in 1999. In the US, the level of trust has also dropped, though not as greatly (from 39.2 percent in 1982 to 35.5 percent in 1999).

According to John Helliwell, Professor Emeritus of Economics at the University of British Columbia, who has analyzed 20 years worth of World Values Survey data, the differences in national average trust have a large and significant effect on reported happiness, and that an increase in national trust levels would lead to an increase in subjective well-being. This is both a remarkable and exciting finding. By finding ways to build more trust in society, between the young and the old, for example, or between different ethnic groups, we can increase our happiness at the same time.

Percentages of populations who believe most people can be trusted

Country	1981	1999
Belgium	25.1	29.4
Canada	47.7	38.4
Denmark	45.9	64.1
France	22.3	21.4
Germany	25.9	31.2
Hungary	31.9	21.4
Italy	24.5	31.8
Japan	37.4	39.6
Netherlands	38.1	59.4
Spain	32.2	36.3
GB	42.5	28.5
USA	39.2	35.5

Poverty

☹ ## 2 POINTS

The United Nations Human Poverty Index ranks all countries according to three basic human needs factors relating to survival, knowledge, and a decent standard of living. At a country level, there is a link between poverty (or wealth) and happiness. So you might be surprised to learn that the most consistent finding from research into individual happiness is that the majority of people are actually quite happy and satisfied with their lives. Using data from over 43 nations, it has been found that the average level of happiness is about 6.75 on a 10 point scale.

Only in two poor nations, India and the Dominican Republic, did the reported level of happiness fall below neutral. In fact, 86 percent of the nations surveyed fall into the positive range, including several less developed countries, such as Thailand, Mexico, Brazil, and Egypt.

Even though slightly different measures of happiness and life satisfaction may have been used in various countries, it's hard to ignore the overall conclusion that most people in the world seem pretty content with their lives. But there is one main exception to this, and that is those people living in abject poverty, who haven't got enough money to meet even the very basic human needs of food, shelter, and providing for their offspring. Not surprisingly the slum dwellers of Calcutta, for example, do experience lower life satisfaction than more affluent comparison groups.

Luck

1 POINT ☺

Are you the sort of person who always seems to be in the right place at the right time? Or are you someone to whom Murphy's Law applies: If anything can go wrong, it will. Do people really attract good and bad fortune, or is something else going on?

Psychologist Professor Richard Wiseman of Hertfordshire University in the UK knows a thing or two about luck, having studied it for well over a decade. According to Wiseman's surveys, 50 percent of people believe they have good luck, 14 percent bad luck, and the rest neither. Wiseman believes that, the lottery apart, luck isn't a purely random phenomenon, nor is it caused by psychic powers or intelligence. Instead, it comes from one's beliefs, and the behaviors connected to them.

Rather than regarding luck as an uncontrollable external factor which doesn't influence our feelings of well-being, psychologists are now speculating that believing in good luck might lead to feelings of optimism, which in turn lead to greater psychological well-being. In other words, according to Wiseman, how you behave can influence how lucky you are. In fact, Wiseman has four simple steps for changing bad luck into good (see box below). Good luck!

How to improve your luck

- Maximize your opportunities.

- Listen to your intuition.

- Expect good luck in the future.

- Look on the positive side of bad luck.

Post-traumatic growth

☺ **1 POINT**

It's estimated that there were some 20 million military and civilian casualties in World War I, escalating to about 70 million in World War II. On top of this millions of soldiers and civilians were injured, plus there was untold misery and suffering caused by those injuries and fatalities, and by the economic hardship which lasted for years afterwards. Even today across the globe there are over 30 ongoing wars and conflicts, which have been responsible for hundreds of thousands of deaths. Why is such grief and sadness relevant in a happiness equation?

The fact is that some people have the capacity to turn the most terrible tragedy around, overcoming extreme hardship, poverty, violence, or torture, not merely restoring their former well-being, but actually improving relationships, achieving a greater appreciation for life, and a greater sense of personal strength as they do so. In spite of, or more accurately, because of, the trauma suffered, they grow and develop as human beings. Thus in a perverse way, trauma can lead to a positive outcome that would not have occurred otherwise. This phenomenon is called post-traumatic growth.

The process of post-traumatic growth relies on making sense of the trauma and then assimilating it into a new view of life. Imagine a beautiful vase that smashes into a hundred tiny pieces. Recreating the vase as it was by gluing the pieces back together will leave it looking nearly the same, but it won't be anywhere near as strong as it was before. Post-traumatic growth is more like creating an entirely new object from the pieces, not a vase, but something equally beautiful, like a mosaic. While tragedy and trauma are obviously not beneficial to our happiness, they can lead to greater physical and psychological health afterwards.

16

Political oppression
2 POINTS ☹

In parts of the world, systematic and violent political oppression in the form of detention, disappearance, murder, torture, and other human rights violations is sanctioned by the state and carried out by secret police forces, military, or paramilitary groups. It is not surprising that living under these sorts of conditions can have a noticeably negative impact on one's happiness and satisfaction with life. In fact, markers of a democratic society such as free and fair elections, freedom of the press, religious freedom, and judicial independence are also important contributors to individual well-being.

People who live in the less developed countries of the world are less happy than those living in the industrially developed nations of America, Australia, and Western Europe. Global surveys, such as the World Values Survey, show that well-being rises in proportion to Gross Domestic Product per capita (see entry 13 on Poverty). In fact, according to research, there are four particular dimensions—social equality, human rights, national income, and individualism—which account for 73 percent of the difference between the average happiness of nations.

So if you live in a stable democracy and are free to choose and pursue your own goals in life, you are likely to be happier.

Collectivist culture

☹ # 2 POINTS

Unlike other animals, humans are 99.9 percent biologically identical; most of the variation that does occur is in the difference between males and females and our unique personality traits. Thus genetically speaking we are more similar than we are different.

An ethnic group, on the other hand, refers to the cultural (and sometimes physical) characteristics used to classify people into groups considered to be significantly different to others. It's no surprise then that when we consider the relationship between ethnicity and happiness, differences do start to emerge, not so much to do with actual levels of well-being and life satisfaction, but with how we're brought up to achieve them.

Bearing in mind that you can be simultaneously happy in one area of your life (e.g., your relationship) and unhappy in another (e.g., your work), research shows that different cultures have different approaches to happiness, emphasizing different goals and values. For example, in individualistic Western countries, happiness is often seen as a reflection of personal achievement. Being unhappy implies that you have not made the most of your life. Meanwhile in the more collectivist nations such as Japan and South Korea, people have a more fatalistic attitude towards happiness. These different attitudes in turn affect how people subjectively report happiness and satisfaction in life. What's more, the things that give people happiness, satisfaction, and meaning in their lives vary considerably between cultures.

Even though different cultural backgrounds influence how different ethnic groups perceive happiness, and how they try to achieve it, subjective well-being is lower in collectivist cultures common in the East (where human interdependence is deemed more important than the individual), than it is in the individualist cultures of the West.

How different cultures report happiness and satisfaction

- Among young Koreans, satisfaction with school contributes more to their overall well-being than it does for young people in the United States, where focusing on one's own goals and independence are more strongly associated with their life satisfaction.

- Japanese workers report much more satisfaction with their work than do American workers. This is thought to be due to the fact that the concept of work is more meaningful for the Japanese than for Americans.

- Surprisingly, the former communist countries of Eastern Europe reported much lower levels of happiness and life satisfaction immediately after democratization than before. Under communist rule, expectations were pretty low, but rose rapidly after democratization. Reality just couldn't keep up.

- Asian Americans, Koreans, and the Japanese pay more attention to positive daily events than do European Americans. Put another way, it takes only 1.3 good events to mitigate 1 bad one for the former, whereas for the latter it takes nearly 2.

Contact with nature

☺ **0.5 POINTS**

After a hectic week at work with meetings, presentations, emails, phone calls, and eating on-the-go, not to mention the hours wasted commuting, it's sheer bliss to get out into the countryside and enjoy being in a green open space. The ancient Chinese practice of feng shui suggests that the design of an environment is particularly important for facilitating positive energy flows, or Qi. Whether or not you believe in feng shui, it's clear that your physical surroundings can have a significant impact on how you feel.

So does contact with nature make you happier? Research shows that people living in environments that lack natural spaces have higher levels of aggression and violence than those living in greener environments. Natural spaces do have a beneficial effect on psychological well-being, such as reducing the mental fatigue caused by tasks that require profound concentration. Views of greenery also have a positive effect on physical health, reducing blood pressure and stress. It also helps hospital patients use fewer painkillers and recover from surgery more quickly.

The reasons why this happens are not entirely clear. It may be that we're particularly drawn to landscapes featuring plants, flowers, and water because they contributed to our survival and reproduction as early humans. Whatever the explanation, there's no doubt that natural environments can make us feel both mentally and physically healthier.

19

Adaptation

2 POINTS ☹

What would you do if you won the lottery? You might buy a new house, maybe give up work to settle down to a life of luxury. And you'd be happier of course, right? Well, actually, no, not necessarily. The curious thing about happiness is that it isn't exactly relative. If it were, all jackpot winners would live happily ever after, and all victims of paralyzing accidents would be miserable for the rest of their lives, but this doesn't happen. The reason, say scientists, is something called the "adaptation effect."

Adaptation works in two ways. Say you did win the lottery—in the short term the simple things that you previously enjoyed, for instance drinking a cool beer on hot summer's day, would seem less satisfying in comparison with the new pleasures that the money brings you. This is called the contrast effect.

In the long term there's also the habituation effect, when the novelty of the good fortune wears off, as it is bound to do. So while you might imagine that winning $1 million will be the answer to all your prayers, science tells us that actually no, you'll just get used to the new pleasures that the extra money brings you. One small glimmer of hope though is that winning a moderate amount on the lottery may reduce your psychological stress one to two years later!

Studies on people who have suffered a terrible misfortune, such as a paralyzing accident, show that the adaptation effect also works for them. Typically they come to terms with the negative event and do not appear nearly as unhappy as you might expect. In fact on a scale of 0 to 5, where 0 is the worst possible thing that could happen in a lifetime and 5 is the best, on average people rated their accident at 1.28.

So where does this leave the millions of people who buy lottery tickets every week? Well, leaving aside any question of whether the odds are worth it, the chances are that if you do win, you probably won't be as happy as you think!

A large part of our happiness is made up of our emotional well-being—not just whether we feel positive or negative today, but whether or not in general we tend to be resilient, curious, optimistic, or simply thankful for the good things which happen in our lives. Often we attribute our emotional well-being to our genes or our personality, so it's tempting to conclude that there is nothing to be done. The problem then is that we think we cannot influence it in any way, whereas given the time, knowledge, and motivation, it is perfectly possible to change one's emotional well-being for the better. So if you tend to be a bit grumpy, the good news is that there's no reason to stay that way!

In this chapter we outline some of the most relevant and useful findings in the major areas of emotional well-being which have been investigated scientifically, and make some suggestions about how you can apply them to your everyday life. So if you feel that your emotional well-being is in need of a boost, dive in!

PART TWO

Emotional Well-being

Negative emotions

☹ # 5 POINTS

Despite being unpleasant, negative emotions play an important role in our lives. Most people have heard of the "fight-or-flight" response, attributed to American physiologist Walter Cannon at the beginning of the 20th century. This connection between feeling and action has an evolutionary benefit: it leads to very specific behaviors: I'm afraid (negative emotion) so I run away (action). So a negative emotion leads to an automatic response, which in a life or death situation, such as being faced by a sabertooth tiger, would have enabled our ancestors to survive.

Negative emotions cause us to focus on a very narrow field of action and minimize distractions. When you're very afraid, for example, you don't stop to think about whether your lipstick is on straight or you've got your wallet, you just run. That's why it's so incredibly difficult to be creative or innovative when you're feeling intensely pressured, and it's much easier to be grouchy and irritable. Studies show that people perform less well on simple tasks, like completing puzzles, when they feel negative. From a work perspective, if you want your team to perform at its best it's crucial to create the kind of environment that discourages negative emotions, or at least nips them in the bud.

Of course, few of us actively welcome negative emotions, although if we understand their presence from an evolutionary perspective it can help. It's useful to remember that we can't dispel them all and we do need some negatives in order to fully appreciate the good things we have!

Negative emotion	Corresponding action
Fear	Escape
Anger	Attack
Disgust	Expel

Feeling good
5 POINTS ☺

Certain bodily pleasures are designed to feel so good that you want them to recur, but do positive emotions, such as joy, rapture, interest, and contentment, have a purpose in the same way as negative emotions?

Positive emotions have at least two fundamental purposes. Psychologist Barbara Fredrickson has suggested that positive emotions expand our attention rather than focus it (as negative emotions do), and in doing so they foster the growth of physical, social, and intellectual resources, which in turn lead to an upward development spiral. So experiencing joy leads us to want to play and be creative, feeling interested leads us to explore and experience, and feeling contented leads us to savor and appreciate.

The second purpose of positive emotions is that they "undo" the effect of negative emotions and enhance resilience and the ability to cope. Humor increases one's tolerance of pain for example. In another study, participants shown positive and uplifting videos after a stressful event or after watching upsetting videos showed faster cardiovascular recovery than did the control group. And in the aftermath of 9/11 resilient people experienced more positive emotions, which led them to feel increased optimism, well-being, and tranquility as well as protecting them against depression.

Lack of confidence

1 POINT

The Oxford English Dictionary defines "confidence" as being self-assured and feeling or showing self-reliance. It suggests that confidence is a trait that you either have or haven't got, like being pessimistic or an extrovert. When asked if they'd like to be more confident, most people say "yes!" Confidence is seen as a highly desirable quality, the lack of which prevents you achieving the things you want to in life.

But the dictionary definition doesn't explain that it's perfectly possible to be self-assured in some parts of your life, and not in others. When you stop to think about it, it's unlikely that you lack confidence in all areas. You may, for example, be a confident parent, lover, and public speaker. And at the same time you may be a less confident cook, swimmer, and mathematician. Confidence has a direct influence on our mental and physical well-being: it impacts how much we persist in the face of difficulties and affects how we feel about ourselves; it can make us more or less vulnerable to stress and depression and it affects the immune system and activates endorphins, our natural pain killers. Confidence is also crucial for people trying to overcome eating disorders or drug abuse—if they don't believe they can, they won't even try. In short, a lack of self-confidence can create a vicious circle.

To build confidence, be specific about the when, where, and how you lack confidence. Then, work to improve that. Don't allow a lack of confidence in a specific area spread to other things.

Self-confidence is a set of beliefs about yourself, not an inherent skill or personality trait. It is very possible to change your confidence level, and it does not have to determine your behavior. You can be very competent and capable, and still feel a lack of self-confidence. It's worthwhile to build your confidence, because some psychologists believe that confidence, along with persistence and effort, is a more powerful determinant of your success than actual innate ability. One of the most effective ways to build confidence is by actually trying to do the thing you think you need confidence for. Expect to feel uncomfortable about being out of your comfort zone at first, and welcome it, because it's a sign that you're learning something new.

So confidence, or the lack of it, isn't fixed, which is good news—it means that we can learn how to become more confident. Athletes, for example, often use imagery to help them build the confidence needed to succeed.

How to build your confidence

- First you need to identify in which areas of your life you would like to have more confidence.

- Be specific about what it is that you want to achieve by improving your confidence.

- Seek support from someone close to you; tell them what you are going to do so that they can encourage you to have more faith in yourself and help you to make bolder choices.

- Break your goal down into small steps so that you can build your confidence gradually, rather than jumping straight in.

- Don't worry about feeling uncomfortable—it's natural to feel awkward as you step outside of your normal comfort zone. Be brave and persevere with your goals.

Powerlessness

3 POINTS

Every year since 1972 the National Opinion Research Center at the University of Chicago has taken the pulse of America through their General Social Survey, which provides invaluable data about the demographic changes in American society. Recently published information on job satisfaction and happiness reveals that it is not salary or conditions which determine how happy people are at work, nor even whether or not their job is a vocation (although all of these things are important). Experts have suggested that the difference between those jobs which give most satisfaction and those which give least is due to whether or not the job occupant feels in control of what they do every day.

This supports studies carried out with nursing home residents in the 1970s, in which it was found that those residents who had some responsibility for their lives lived longer and were happier than those whose decisions were all made for them.

How can feeling in control of your destiny benefit your well-being? If you believe that what you do makes a difference to how your life turns out then you're more likely to work for achievements, postpone gratification, set long-term goals, tolerate anxiety, benefit more from social support, and spend more time studying and preparing for tests, thereby achieving more academically.

Research also shows that feeling in control buffers against stress and negative emotions, and increases energy and vigor. Furthermore, people who have higher levels of perceived control take greater responsibility for their health.

So all in all, being in control of your life is a key contributor to your overall health and happiness.

Vitality

1 POINT ☺

Vitality is associated with greater subjective well-being and good physical health. Because it's an active positive state, it differs from happiness, which can include the passive states of contentment and satisfaction. Virtually any factor that affects psychological and physical health also influences vitality—for example, depression, anxiety, and stress. On top of this, health-related lifestyle choices, such as smoking, poor diet, and lack of physical exercise can also result in lower vitality.

Although stimulants such as caffeine and recreational drugs will artificially boost your energy levels, the affect doesn't last, may not be positive, and can lead to other health problems.

Similarly, eating sugary snacks will initially boost energy and decrease tiredness but two hours later, energy levels will have decreased and tiredness increased beyond what they were initially.

Vitality boosters	Vitality drainers to avoid
• Eat a balanced diet.	• Drinking alcohol.
• Exercise regularly.	• Eating a poor diet (or one low in iron).
• Get a good night's sleep.	• Irregular mealtimes.
• Go for a walk in the fresh air.	• Poor sleep.
• Participate in creative arts or music.	• Lack of physical exercise.
• Laugh.	• Physical injury or chronic pain.
• If you've been sitting down for a long time, get up and move around.	• Depression, anxiety, and stress.

Positive illusions

☺ **2 POINTS**

It's intriguing that most normal individuals have a tendency to see themselves in an enhanced, rather than a truly realistic, way. For example, when asked how accurately a list of positive and negative traits describes their personality, most people tend to say that the positive attributes are more characteristic than the negative ones.

Most people also recall positive information about their personality more easily than negative information, show better recall of successes than failures, and tend to remember their performance at various tasks as more positive than it was in reality. In addition, people tend to consider the things they are good at as more important than the things they are not so good at, and dismiss their negative characteristics as inconsequential. Most people will say they are a better than average driver, for example, even though logically this is impossible!

Rather than being the sign of an egotistical or self-important person, or of someone who is not in touch with reality, this type of "self-deception" is a perfectly normal and healthy quality. In fact, there is evidence that individuals who are low in self-esteem or moderately depressed have more accurate self-perceptions!

So what's the purpose of seeing oneself in an unrealistically positive light? Well, studies suggest that positive illusions are important for maintaining a sense of well-being and preserving self-esteem, plus they make it easier for us to make friends and bond with each other. Positive illusions may also make us more creative and productive, as well as increasing our motivation and ability to persist at difficult tasks. These are all very good reasons to start thinking highly of yourself.

Curiosity

1 POINT ☺

Curiosity is a curious word, having both favorable and unfavorable connotations. Typically in its positive sense we think of it as an eager desire to know or learn about something. It's a characteristic that has driven explorers, scientists, artists, and inventors of every nation to great achievements for centuries. On the other hand its negative sense can refer to a preference for novelty or thrill seeking, which could lead to risky behavior, for example, using illegal drugs.

Sticking with the benign form of curiosity, we know that it stimulates positive emotions and thus happiness. Inquisitive and interested people are more creative, feel less stress and boredom, and enjoy challenges both at work and outside. Curious children enjoy school more, have better relationships with their teachers, and have the belief that they will achieve. In terms of interpersonal relationships, highly curious individuals experience greater intimacy and attraction.

So is it possible to develop your sense of curiosity? As yet there aren't any scientifically researched exercises which do this, although it has been suggested that open-ended education in schools (for example, learning about the history of World War II by talking to veterans rather than just reading about it) may generate both short and long-term curiosity. Supportive environments and finding an activity personally meaningful both influence how curious you are. So if you're a teacher or a boss, make sure your kids or employees feel safe and secure, since this is likely to foster curiosity, and lead to an upward spiral of positive emotion.

Depression

☹ # 5 POINTS

According to World Health Organization experts, depression (by which we mean the debilitating mental condition which prevents us from carrying out normal daily activities for at least a few weeks, as opposed to the spells of sadness or distress that we all naturally feel from time to time) is on the increase across the world and by 2020 it will become the second largest cause of suffering after heart disease.

It is estimated that between 5 and 10 percent of the global population at any given time is suffering from identifiable depression, requiring medical treatment or psychosocial intervention; the life-time risk of developing it is 10 to 20 percent for women and slightly less for men. The impact on individuals, families, and society as a whole is enormous—depression is estimated to cost the US economy more than $43 billion annually in medical treatment and lost productivity. And despite this, only 30 percent of the cases worldwide are properly diagnosed and treated, meaning that depression is probably the largest single cause of unhappiness in the world.

According to recent research, depression is associated with the presence of one form of the 5-HTTLPR gene, which when activated by highly stressful life events, can lead to full-blown depression. But even if you are unfortunate enough to have this gene, you needn't think you are destined to live an unhappy life. Depression can be avoided by steering clear of stressful situations, and, if this isn't possible, by actively seeking medical or psychotherapeutic interventions (like Cognitive Behavioral Therapy) at the appropriate time. In this way, you can improve your chances of living a happy and fulfilling life, despite your genes.

28

Humility
1 POINT ☺

Humility is a characteristic we commonly associate with being humble, having a low opinion of oneself, being meek, lacking in self-esteem, or of little worth. The idea doesn't really fit well in highly competitive economies, particularly Capitalist ones.

But humility is a much more interesting attribute than that. It's defined by psychologists, sociologists, theologians, and some philosophers as having, firstly, an accurate, but not low, opinion of yourself and, secondly, the ability to keep your talents and achievements in perspective. What's more, being humble involves giving up the inclination to focus on yourself, becoming instead ever-more open to the importance, worth, and potential of people around you. Evidence is now beginning to emerge that you can be both a humble and a highly successful individual. Not only that, but humility is believed to be linked to increased happiness and well-being through a number of different pathways (see box).

How humility affects happiness

- Increased optimism.

- Improved friendships and intimate relationships.

- Greater satisfaction and morale at work.

- Openness to new experiences and new learning.

- Greater empathy, compassion, and altruism.

- Decreased anxiety, fear, and depression.

- Decreased conflict, anger, and aggression.

29

Pessimism

☹ # 4 POINTS

Generally speaking if you're a pessimist you've drawn the short straw when it comes to happiness. People who see the world in a "glass half empty" way tend to cope by denying that a problem exists, or by disengaging in some way and not resolving the issue. Pessimists are generally more doubtful and hesitant than optimists, and expect the worst to happen. When the worst does happen, this merely confirms that they were right to think pessimistically and thus the negative thinking pattern is reinforced. Not surprisingly, pessimists suffer more anxiety and depression when faced with difficulties than their optimistic cousins do.

If you think you're a pessimist, it isn't all doom and gloom. A small proportion of people use defensive pessimism as a beneficial coping strategy. This involves setting unrealistically low expectations to help prepare for the worst, even when previous performance has been good. So for example, some students automatically expect to do badly in an exam, even when they have previously done well. They mentally rehearse all the possible bad outcomes. Rather than sending them into a spiral of negativity, this pessimistic behavior allows the students to avoid getting caught up in their emotions and in fact enables them to act more effectively, for example, by doing more studying.

Defensive pessimists do best when they are allowed to think through all the possible negative outcomes, rather than think optimistically about what might happen. One study with darts players showed that they performed better when they imagined all the things that could go wrong, rather than when they thought about positive things. But being an optimist has many of its own benefits, so if you would like to learn how to reverse pessimism and be more optimistic, see the box on the opposite page.

Optimism

5 POINTS ☺

Are you a "glass half full" person? The type who looks on the bright side of life, rather than worry over all the what-might-have-beens or what-ifs? If so, this is very good news for both your mental and physical well-being. Research has shown that when dealing with difficulties in their lives, optimistic people experience less distress, anxiety, and depression than do pessimistic people.

Optimists learn from negative events, they persist longer at difficult tasks, and tend not to give up, assuming that the situation can be handled one way or another. Optimistic surgery patients experience less hostility and depression before surgery, and greater relief, happiness, and satisfaction with medical aftercare. A study of life insurance salespeople found that the top 10 percent of optimists outsold the bottom 10 percent of pessimists by an incredible 88 percent.

But optimists don't necessarily see the world through rose-colored glasses. There is evidence that they heed health warnings and take action, rather than sticking their heads in the sand. They eat better and have more regular medical check ups, leading to physical well-being.

How to become more optimistic

1. Build awareness of your Automatic Negative Thoughts (ANTs). Wear an elastic band on your wrist and snap it every time you think something negative.

2. When things go wrong, dispute any pessimistic explanations you have—what other possible explanations could there be? What would it be more useful to believe? Disputation becomes easier with practice.

3. Deliberately put aside worrisome thoughts until later—this leaves you free to act in the present.

Resilience

☺ **4 POINTS**

Have you ever wondered how why some people seem to bounce back from adversity, whether serious illness, bankruptcy, physical assault, or other trauma, whereas others succumb to depression and go under? What is it about resilient people that enables them to pull through successfully, and in some cases, do even better than before?

For example, one person facing bankruptcy might face his problems head on; rather than simply giving up in the face of adversity, this person would work hard to build up a new business from scratch, even more determined to succeed than before. On the other hand, another person might not deal so well with a negative event, for example a mugging, so despite having recovered physically, will no longer go out of the house, and has given up work completely.

So what makes people respond differently to their misfortunes? Researchers believe that thinking style, optimism, temperament, self-control, and sense of humor all contribute to the probability of being able to bounce back, as do a positive family environment and supportive relationships.

Happiness also enhances resilience, creating what's known as a virtuous circle. A study of the after-effects of 9/11 found that resilient people experience more positive emotions, and that positive emotions protect from depression and lead to increased optimism, well-being, and tranquility.

32

Acceptance

1 POINT ☺

In psychological terms, acceptance is the experience of a (usually problematic) situation without trying to change it. It's not the same thing as "giving up" or "doing nothing," however, since it's also possible to take no action on a situation, and at the same time not accept it emotionally. Acceptance could be described in terms of not searching for an answer to problematic situations and focusing instead on other positive aspects of your everyday life. Research suggests that acceptance often leads to a re-evaluation of personal goals and priorities.

Often we talk about acceptance in terms of negative life experiences, such as bereavement, infidelity, and ill health. In practical terms, it means being willing to experience typically uncomfortable thoughts and feelings without letting them dictate your behavior. But what has this got to do with happiness? In research on people with chronic fatigue syndrome, the experience of acceptance had a positive effect on both the fatigue and the psychological aspects of well-being, even after other factors were controlled. Studies on people with chronic pain syndrome showed that acceptance of chronic pain, as opposed to merely coping with the condition, was associated with less pain, disability, depression, and anxiety and with better work status. And in workplace studies, acceptance has been shown to predict both mental and physical well-being, although not job satisfaction.

These findings suggest that you may be happier if you learn how to accept, rather than how to cope with, a negative situation, whether it be a physical health issue or a psychological one.

33

Stress

☹ # 4 POINTS

According to the UK's Health and Safety Executive, workplace stress is the biggest cause of sickness absence in the UK, with a total of 13.8 million workdays lost due to stress, anxiety, and depression in 2006 and 2007. In America, the situation is no better. The National Institute of Occupational Safety and Health reports that up to 40 percent of workers say they are stressed at work, and work problems are more strongly associated with health complaints than any other life stressor.

It's been long established that living or working in a stressful environment can have a negative impact on physical and psychological health. Stress causes your heart rate, blood pressure, and level of cortisol to increase, an automatic evolutionary reaction which we also know as the "flight or fight response" (see entry 20). The physical effects of stress are not only short-term. Research shows that raised cortisol levels lead to premature aging of the brain, and change the fats in the blood. Put this together with raised blood pressure, and the risk of you succumbing to a heart attack or stroke increases enormously. It makes sense from a health perspective to minimize the stress you feel day-to-day.

In the short term there are many things that you can do to help lower your stress, some of which are bad for you in other ways; such as smoking, drinking, overeating, and taking drugs. These might make you feel better in the moment, but often lead to further problems. On the other hand yoga, meditation, physical exercise, and creative activities such as watercolor painting (see entry 49) will all help to ease stress, although they won't eradicate it for ever. In the longer term, you need to act on the source of the stress itself.

The first step is to identify what is causing the stress and then work out what you can do about it. Sometimes it's possible to find a solution yourself; when it comes to the work environment, you might have to negotiate with your employer in order to reach a mutually beneficial outcome. Whatever action you decide to take, remember that new activities and behaviors take time to settle in, so be prepared not to see the benefit immediately. Similarly, new behaviors, even if they're more healthy ones, may also create adverse side affects. For example, if you're a married working father, enrolling in a weekly yoga class after work will mean that you have less time to spend with the family. So it's worth discussing planned changes with your nearest and dearest, to agree how you can maximize the benefits for all.

How to relieve stress

- Use relaxation techniques such as meditation (see entry 97).

- Practice slow breathing using the lower part of your lungs.

- Talk to someone supportive.

- Go for a walk or take physical exercise.

- Take up a relaxing hobby such as watercolor painting.

- Accept practical help from friends/colleagues.

- Let off steam—e.g., go where no one can hear you and scream, or hit a cushion or use a stress ball.

- Know your limits—walk away from ultra-stressful situations until you have regained control.

- Take a vacation.

- Tackle unhelpful addictions like drugs, smoking, and alcohol.

Poor time management

☹ **1 POINT**

Twenty or thirty years ago, trend watchers predicted that by the turn of the new century we'd all have far more leisure time at our disposal, largely due to technological changes. Ironically, for many of us in the Western world, the opposite seems to have happened. Work-life balance has become an organizational mantra in the last decade. We definitely seem busier than we used to be!

So it's strange when we look at the data to find that in actual fact we have on average between five and seven hours more free time per week than we did in 1965. When people are asked to guess how much free time they have, typically they misjudge it by as much as 50 percent, estimating that they have about 20 leisure hours a week when in fact they have 40. So why do we always seem to be so busy?

If you're employed, the chances are you've been to a time management course at some point in your career, where you were taught all sorts of little tricks for how to make better use of your time, most of which probably haven't made the slightest difference. In fact research shows that time management training has very little effect on our performance or on how effectively we use our time. What matters, as it turns out, is motivation, whether we have a choice about the things we do, and whether we have a proactive or reactive approach to time.

It's worth remembering that the most consistent difference between people who are happy with their time use and those who aren't is that the happy ones regularly take time out for themselves.

Too much choice

5 POINTS ☹

It's a commonly held belief that more choice leads to greater freedom, which then leads to greater well-being and that as a result, more choice means greater well-being. On the face of it, this makes perfect sense, doesn't it? Some choice is good for you, it gives you autonomy and enables you to exercise control over your life, even if it's as simple as what to wear when you get up in the morning, or as important as what career to follow. So it seems perfectly logical that more choice must be better for you. But is choice always a good thing?

Research suggests that while some choice has a beneficial effect on our well-being, too much choice is bad for us. Being overloaded with choices results in the complete inability to choose, feelings of regret, raised expectations, and blaming oneself when the chosen option turns out to be less than perfect.

How to make choices

- Learn to spend careful time over a choice only when it is worth it, for example, choosing a career, but not a new mobile phone.

- For unimportant decisions try to be satisfied with an option that is merely good enough, rather than trying to make absolutely the best choice.

- Lower your expectations—do not expect perfection, no matter how many choices there are.

- Try to stick to your choices and don't change your mind.

- Once you've made up your mind, stop looking at the alternatives!

Gratitude

☺ # 5 POINTS

As a child you probably remember having to write thank-you letters for birthday and Christmas presents. As an adult it's probably not something you do as frequently, if at all. It's not that you're not thankful for the things you have in life, just that you don't often stop to think about it.

In fact, expressing your gratitude for something or someone, whether in writing or verbally, is one of the simplest but most effective ways of increasing your happiness. There is overwhelming empirical evidence that people with a grateful disposition are more enthusiastic, joyful, attentive, determined, interested, helpful, optimistic, and energetic than those who aren't. Not only that, but grateful people have been shown to be less depressed, anxious, lonely, envious, and materialistic. In an Internet sample of over 5000 adults, gratitude was one of the top five character strengths consistently and robustly associated with life satisfaction. Studies show that doing gratitude exercises like the two examples below everyday for a couple of weeks can really boost your well-being.

How to express your gratitude

1. Write a gratitude letter. Think of someone who has been kind to you, or helped you in some way, to whom you have never expressed your thanks. It might be a parent, friend, colleague or teacher. Write them a letter, describing what they did and what effect it had on you.

2. At the end of each day, write down three good things that went well for you. These can be significant or relatively unimportant events, it doesn't matter. For each thing, reflect on why it went well. You might like to share your three good things with a partner.

Unhappy endings
2 POINTS ☹

Common sense suggests that, generally, we try to maximize our happiness and minimize our unhappiness. It would seem sensible that the length of a positive or negative experience would also impact how we feel about it and how we remember it. A two week vacation is surely twice as good as a one week vacation in the same place, assuming that the intensity of the positive experience is the same in both instances. Equally for a negative experience, a 20-minute root canal procedure must be twice as bad as a ten minute one, assuming the same intensity of pain.

But things aren't so straightforward. Our memory of an event is affected by the peak experience and by how the event ends (the "peak end" rule), rather than by how long it lasts. A one week vacation marred by atrocious weather but which ended with a fantastic party would be remembered more favorably than one in which the sun shone throughout but which ended in you having your wallet stolen.

In an experiment, one group of patients undergoing a colonoscopy exam had the colonoscope left in place for another minute after the exam, thus adding a mildly uncomfortable experience which, though less preferred than removing it altogether, was not as uncomfortable as the preceding exam. The other group had the colonoscope removed immediately after the exam was over. The first group provided higher evaluations of the procedure than the second group, even though their total discomfort lasted longer. The difference was that they recalled the experience ending on a slightly more positive note because the pain slowly decreased rather than just stopping abruptly.

Often we have to do things we don't want to do—visiting relatives in the hospital, or giving a presentation at work. In these cases, try to see how you can ensure that the experience ends on a high, since this is what you will remember.

Forgiveness

☺ # 2 POINTS

We tend to believe that the act of forgiving has a huge emotional and psychological "cost" for the victim, without any gain, hence the reason it's so difficult to do. At the same time, we intuitively know that bearing grudges is also harmful—we often talk about being unable to "let go" of past hurts, for example. But what if we take the perspective that forgiveness is something that you do for yourself and not for the person who has wronged you?

Evidence is slowly emerging to support the perspective that forgiving is good for your well-being. Studies show that the act of forgiving reduces anger, hostility, depression, anxiety, and negative emotions. In addition, forgiving people are more likely to be happier, more agreeable, and more serene. Forgiveness is also linked to physical health benefits such as a reduction in blood pressure levels and it may aid in cardiovascular recovery from stress. On the other hand, nursing grudges or dwelling on revenge not only prevents you moving on, it also prompts higher levels of anger and sadness and a significantly higher heart rate and blood pressure.

How to enhance your forgiving side

- Write a letter of forgiveness (you don't have to send it).

- Forgive yourself for a past transgression.

- Read about public figures who have practiced forgiveness such as Nelson Mandela or Mahatma Gandhi.

- Imagine forgiving a wrongdoer, and how much better you feel as a result.

- Practice empathizing in your daily life— don't jump to conclusions if someone does something you don't understand.

Coping well

2 POINTS ☺

At some point in our lives all of us will have to cope with misfortune and crises. Psychologists have identified three different ways we can respond to a problem: we can actively try to solve it; deal with the emotions we feel; or distract ourselves and pretend it doesn't exist. Each of these ways can be beneficial or detrimental to our health and happiness, depending how we go about it.

If trying to find a solution to the problem, it's important that you accept responsibility, develop a realistic plan, and remain optimistic. If you procrastinate, remain pessimistic, or don't follow plans through, the chances are that nothing changes, or the situation may deteriorate, leaving you worse off than before.

The same applies to dealing with painful emotions—for example, calling on good friends for support, or turning to relaxation or exercise. Research shows that relaxation enables us to cope better with stress, anxiety, and pain while exercise reduces feelings of depression and releases endorphins in the brain, resulting in a sense of well-being. Catharsis can also be a beneficial form of emotional coping; studies show that people who write about their traumas have better immune systems, better health, and pay fewer visits to the doctor than those who write about unimportant topics. However, there are also non-beneficial forms of emotional coping, such as seeking meaningless spiritual support (such as visiting a fortune teller), taking drugs, drinking, or engaging in unproductive wishful thinking.

Avoiding the issue altogether can have some advantages—particularly where it allows us some time to marshal our resources in the short term. Listening to music or taking a long warm bath can be good ways to wind down and give yourself some breathing room. Ignoring a problem long term, however, is not good for your well-being—often the problem can persist or even get worse.

Fixed mindset

☹ ## 2 POINTS

Do you believe that your intellect, ability, and potential are carved in stone? Do you label yourself (or your children) as sporty, musical, clever, arty, good at languages, or not? If so, the chances are that you have what Stanford University psychologist, Carol Dweck, calls a "fixed mindset." If you pass an exam with flying colors or win a golf tournament it's a reflection of your intelligence or talent. If you don't, on the other hand, it means that your basic qualities are inadequate and you'll feel anxious as a result. Everything you do is framed in terms of performance, which can be measured and validated by yourself and by others. Dweck's research has found that fixed mindset people frequently pass up the chance to improve their abilities for two reasons: firstly, because they don't believe that trying will make a difference and secondly, because having to try proves that they aren't capable in the first place! It's a no-win situation!

Having a fixed mindset means that you have to keep succeeding in order to feel good about yourself. Take the former top-ranked tennis player, the legendary John McEnroe. Remember the way he responded when things didn't go his way? Dweck suggests that McEnroe suffered from a fixed mindset, which prevented him learning from mistakes.

Dweck has identified the existence of a much more helpful frame of mind, called the "growth mindset," in which people believe that their capabilities and potential can be enhanced and developed through practice and effort. It's based on the fact that the human brain is an organ that continues to grow throughout our lives as we learn new things. For example, the auditory cortex of a musician's brain grows denser than that of a non-musician because of all the new neural connections made through musical practice. The more we learn the more connections are made in the brain, and the denser our brain grows. So it makes much more sense to adopt a "growth mindset," one which allows you to try new ways of doing things if the first, second, or third attempt fails. The goals of growth mindset people are about learning and competence, not performance, so whether they succeed or fail, they'll still learn something new from the experience. Even better news is that learning goals have been shown to increase performance and enjoyment, and decrease negative emotion at the same time.

How to develop a growth mindset

- Remember that the brain, like any other human muscle, gets stronger the more you use it.

- Listen out for your "fixed mindset voice"—the one that criticizes you for not succeeding, urges you to give up in the face of a setback, or which says, "if you were good enough you wouldn't have to try."

- Recognize that it's up to you how you interpret challenges and setbacks. You can see them as signs that you don't have the necessary skill or ability, or that you need to stretch yourself and try harder.

- When times get tough, remember that people are successful because they persist. Even authors like John Grisham and J.K. Rowling were rejected by many publishers before finally getting a deal.

- Learn from setbacks—pick yourself up and try again.

Worrying

☹ # 5 POINTS

Are you a chronic worrier or "overthinker?" Perhaps you believe that focussing on the minutiae of a situation will somehow enlighten you, give insight or provide the answer to your problem.

Well actually, overthinking can make you feel even more pessimistic and self-critical, as well as undermining your motivation and concentration. It can create distorted thinking patterns and can ultimately lead to full-blown depression. As it also demands a great deal of mental energy, there is little left over for more creative or helpful thinking patterns. But you can learn to overcome it as shown below.

How to escape the over-thinking trap

1. Loosen the overthinking ties:

a) Imagine a large red "Stop" sign.

b) Distract yourself.

c) Set aside 30 minutes a day specifically for worrying, and only worry then.

d) Talk to a trusted friend who can help you dispute your thoughts.

e) Write your negative thoughts down.

2. Take action—every small step you take to solve the problem will be a step towards greater well-being.

3. Avoid overthinking traps—write a list of the specific triggers for your over-thinking (e.g., specific times of the day or places) and avoid them in future.

4. Ask yourself whether what you are worrying about will really matter in a year's time. If the answer is "yes," then focus your thinking on what you can learn from the experience.

Positive time perceptions

3 POINTS ☺

Scientists have discovered that the way we perceive time can make a huge difference to our levels of happiness. Time perspective is divided into three broad categories—past, present, and future. You will tend to have just one dominant one.

Studies show that "past" people can focus in either a positive and sentimental way, or in a negative way. The former group have good relationships with family and friends, and fond memories; but the latter feel haunted by their past, focussing on unpleasant experiences, and feeling bitter as a result. "Here and now" people might "seize the day" but are at greater risk from temptations such as alcohol and drugs, which can affect their long-term happiness. A "present fatalist" is more likely to feel that outside forces control their life and thus experience feelings of helplessness and hopelessness. "Future oriented" people delay current gratification and focus on goals and rewards. They tend to be more successful than others, but risk becoming workaholics, and neglect social relationships.

So which of the three is the most likely to lead to happiness? Research shows that those who have a "positive past" perspective are the happiest; but even this can lead to problems such as being overly cautious, avoiding new experiences, and maintaining the status quo even when it's not in your best interest.

Experts suggest that a balanced time perspective—adapting your outlook to your current situation—affords the most advantages. So when you're playing with the kids or on vacation, focus on the present, enjoy the moment and don't let other issues encroach. At work, focus on being as productive as possible and put other problems out of your mind. And when thinking about your past, acceptance (see entry 32) and forgiveness (see entry 38) are crucial to your happiness—don't let old hurts and mistakes spoil your chance for happiness today.

Comparing yourself

☹ **5 POINTS**

We wouldn't be human if we didn't occasionally compare ourselves with other people. Particularly in target-driven societies the comparison habit seems to start in school (who came top of the class in math? Are you wearing designer sneakers or knockoffs?) and it never really stops. It's fine to make the occasional comparison with friends, neighbors or colleagues; it might even spur you on to greater achievement yourself when you see someone else doing something brilliantly.

The problem comes when we do it too frequently or when we compare ourselves to those who are clearly not in our reference group, which is all too likely now given the prevalence of advertising on TV, in magazines, on billboards, and the Internet. Upward comparison with people who earn three, five, or ten times our salaries or more can only lead to greater dissatisfaction and lower happiness as we make a judgment and find ourselves lacking in some way. Let's face it, there will always be someone who is more beautiful, more intelligent, slimmer, richer, or healthier than us!

Part of the problem with comparison arises because of the reference group we choose. Take bronze and silver Olympic medalists for example. Logic says that

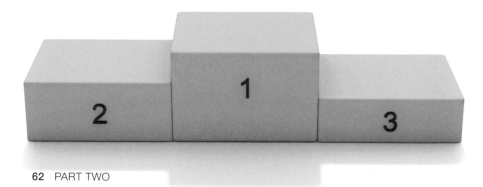

silver medalists would be happier than bronze winners, but in fact it's the latter who are happier. The reason is that bronze medalists tend to compare themselves to the athletes who didn't win a medal at all whereas the silver medalists believe they might have won gold if only they'd tried harder.

Happy and unhappy people approach social comparison in different ways. It's not that happy people don't make comparisons; they do. However, other people's successes and failures don't diminish or augment their own. Unhappy people on the other hand feel bad when they see that someone else is more successful (in whatever avenue) than they are; it can make them feel inferior, envious, or resentful, as well as lowering their self-esteem.

How to survive social comparison

1. Acknowledge that there will always be someone better off in some way than you.

2. Notice who your reference group is—are you behaving like a bronze or a silver medalist?

2. Notice when you start to make upward comparisons and distract yourself with another activity.

3. Avoid situations that lead to comparison, for instance, stop buying celebrity magazines or newspaper "rich lists."

4. Put it in perspective—will whatever you are concerned about now matter when you're on your deathbed?

Happiness isn't just about emotional well-being; physical well-being has a significant part to play too. It s not all about how physically healthy you actually are either. How healthy you think you are is what really counts as you ll see in entry 4.

If you're a sporty person, you ve got a bit of head start in the race to achieve greater physical well-being, but even if you re not, there are still plenty of things that you can do which will contribute greatly to your happiness. The suggestions that have been included here all have some scientific evidence to support them. Some, like dancing, will be appropriate for people who are very active; others, like gardening, can be adapted to suit your mobility. There are suggestions for those who want to get out (visiting a gallery) and for those who want to stay in (writing a diary). Whatever your level of physical mobility, finding a hobby which totally absorbs you is essential to your well-being.

PART THREE

Physical Well-being

Finding the flow

☺ # 5 POINTS

What do athletes, actors, and artists commonly do which improves their performance, and which you can also do? Well, have you ever noticed how musicians often seem to get lost in their music, eyes closed, as if in a trance-like state? This is known as "flow" and it occurs when you're so fully absorbed in what you're doing that you don't notice what's going on around you. You often lose track of time, and afterwards you feel great. Athletes call it "being in the zone."

In order to be able to get into a flow state with your favorite activity, the levels of challenge and skill need to be in equilibrium. The important point about flow is that it's a tried and tested pathway to achieving greater happiness, through controlling your inner experience or consciousness. What activities lead you to become completely absorbed and not self-conscious? What works for you may be different to what works for your partner or your work colleagues. But the more you get into flow, the happier you'll feel!

How to improve your chances of finding flow

- Make sure the activity has clear goals.

- Concentrate on what you're doing.

- Choose an activity in which you get direct feedback about what you are doing well or not so well so that you can change what you do as needed.

- Make sure that the activity is pitched at the right level of challenge (neither too easy nor too difficult).

- If the activity is too easy, find a way to make it more challenging.

- If it's too hard, find a way to boost your skill level.

Lack of exercise

5 POINTS ☹

While the definition of what counts as physical exercise (i.e., moderate or strenuous activity?) varies depending on which expert you speak to, all health professionals agree that doing some form of exercise on a regular basis is essential for keeping the mind as well as the body fit and healthy. In one Finnish study, people who exercised at least twice a week experienced significantly less depression, anger, distrust, and stress, felt more in control of their health, more socially integrated, and felt their lives were more meaningful than those who exercised less frequently or not at all.

In the USA, roughly 62 percent of adults engage in at least some physical activity during their leisure time. This means that 38 percent don't engage in any physical activity whatsoever! And participation levels decrease as people get older. It's a similar story in the UK and Australia. Statistics for Europe published in 2002 showed that just under 40 percent of all adults answered yes when asked, "do you exercise at least twice a week," which means that a staggering 60 percent don't. Of course, the figures range enormously by country: in Ireland the proportion of people who don't exercise was 34 percent, while in Greece it reached 80 percent.

So in the industrialized world at least, it looks like we're a bunch of couch potatoes, despite mounting evidence that exercise can mitigate against psychological as well as physical illness. In one study, participants diagnosed with depression were randomly assigned to medication, exercise, or a combination. Ten months later recurrence rates for the medication only group were 38 percent, for the combination group 31 percent and for the exercise only group 9 percent. The message here is that physical exercise is an absolute must for not only your physical health but also your mental well-being.

Watching TV

🙁 **4 POINTS**

The good news is that leisure time for the average American has increased by 6.2 hours a week for men and 4.9 hours a week for women between 1965 and 2003; the bad news is that the majority of this extra free time is consumed by that monster in the corner of the room (or on the wall, if you're high tech), the television.

For some people, TV viewing can be a social bonding experience, if not at the time then round the water cooler at work the next day, as we swap stories about what we watched. For others though, especially in the Western world, watching television is probably the biggest waste of free time ever.

The average American watches almost 5 hours of TV a day, and Europeans don't fare much better, watching on average 3 hours a day. It's easy to conclude that watching TV must make us happy, or why else would we do it so frequently and for so long?

It's true that, all things being equal, people who watch less than half an hour of TV a day are more satisfied with their lives than people who watch more. Research suggests that TV rarely portrays reality (even the so-called "reality" shows) — in fact on the whole TV programs show much more violence, unstable relationships, more affluent people, and more luxury than there is in real life.

So people who watch a lot of television tend to overestimate crime rates, and are therefore more fearful and anxious; they are less trusting of other people and don't socialize as much as peers who don't watch a lot of TV; they also tend to overestimate other people's wealth, place more importance on material goods, and are less satisfied with their income.

On top of this, TV viewing, for most of us, is a passive activity which doesn't require any skill; you just turn it on and use the remote to flick from channel to channel. As a result we can easily become apathetic and bored. All these factors contribute to lower subjective well-being. The one exception is for blind and deaf people, who can experience flow when watching TV, because it requires much more skill to interpret what is happening without the pictures or sound.

It's worth pointing out however that we don't know whether the type of program we choose makes a difference. It's easy to imagine that time spent watching a natural history program or a quiz might be educational, but would nonstop documentaries about the realities of life really make us feel better?

The chances are that doing something else with your time, like going for a run or calling a friend, will have a more beneficial effect on your well-being.

How to moderate your viewing habits

- Don't watch TV every night and don't switch the TV on the minute you get through the door.

- Once your show has finished, switch off the TV, don't channel-surf.

- If you've got kids, plan an evening of fun family activities instead.

- Be mindful of the choices you're making. Select the programs you want to watch at the start of the week and stick to them.

- Take up a new hobby with all the spare time you've now got!

Dancing

☺ **3 POINTS**

When was the last time you put on your fancy clothes, let your hair down, and hit the dance floor? Your cousin's wedding, or the office Christmas party? It's fantastic for keeping you physically healthy: US research shows that a vigorous dance class can burn as many calories as a gym workout, while a study of older people found that dancing significantly improved levels of unhealthy fats in the blood.

There are many other benefits to dancing though—it increases your strength and stamina, tones your leg and buttock muscles, increases your lung capacity, and learning new routines also keeps your brain sharp. And practicing your pirouettes or finessing your fandango is a lot more fun than the treadmill!

In addition to the physical benefits, there is growing evidence that dancing is good for your psychological health. Dance and movement therapy is based on the premise that mind and body are interconnected with the result that expressing yourself through bodily movement may have a secondary effect on your mental and emotional well-being.

Recent studies show that hip-hop dancing has a more positive impact on well-being than either ice-skating or body conditioning, and that afterwards psychological distress and fatigue are lower. You may experience improved self-esteem and communication from taking part in aerobic dancing, as well as heightened feelings of well-being and a sense of accomplishment.

So whether you're into hip-hop, disco, ballet, line, folk, or tap, you can be sure that dancing contributes enormously to both your mental and your physical fitness.

48

Gardening
3 POINTS ☺

Gardening is no longer seen merely in terms of growing prize chrysanthemums for the local produce show or tending a weed free lawn. Now it's an opportunity for personal growth, self-expression, and finding meaning. Traditionally considered a hobby for the staid and unadventurous, these days the restorative and creative powers of gardening are being revealed to the public at large through the arrival of so-called "lifestyle" TV programs accompanied by a new and eclectic species of TV show host called the Celebrity Gardener.

What all these famous gardeners would agree on is that there's nothing quite like getting outside and getting your hands dirty, planting, digging, watering, harvesting, and pruning. Or maybe just looking, relaxing, and enjoying, absorbing the abundance of colors, textures, and scents, appreciating being so close to nature. If you're a green thumb yourself you won't be in the least bit surprised to hear that, according to research, regular gardening helps keep you physically healthy, specifically reducing heart disease and cholesterol levels, improving diabetes care, manual dexterity, and coordination skills.

Possibly because plants require active nurturing in order to grow, studies also show that gardening greatly benefits your mental health, decreasing stress and depression, and increasing self-esteem, resulting in a significant improvement in positive emotion and psychological well-being. So whether you've got a window box, a handful of containers, a small yard or an acre of prime soil at your fingertips, get your rubber clogs on and go out there and get gardening!

Having a hobby

☺ **4 POINTS**

Many people these days complain about the long hours they work and consequently how little time they have to do the things they love, whether it's playing with the kids, taking salsa lessons, collecting Elvis Presley memorabilia or researching family history. Whatever your hobby, we're pretty sure that you'd prefer to spend more time on it than on your work: remember that quotation, "nobody ever said on their deathbed, 'I wish I'd spent more time in the office'."

It's an interesting fact that we believe that we work longer hours than ever before, whereas statistics show that for most of us over the past 30 or 40 years our leisure time has increased. American men, for example, have on average an extra 6.2 hours of leisure time a week. For UK men aged 25-44, the average amount of time spent working fell by 25 minutes per day between 2000 and 2005. For the average French person, daily free time increased by 18 minutes a day between 1986 and 1999.

Studies of time use and time perspectives reveal that the amount of time needed to spend on leisure activities in order to feel satisfied varies greatly from person to person. For some of us, spending a couple of hours on our hobby every other weekend is enough to recharge our batteries. But for others even as much as a couple of hours a day leaves us wanting more. Then there are those of us whose interests become our work—photographers for example, or professional soccer players. If you keep your work and leisure well and truly separate, the trick is to find the right balance. If on the one hand you pursue your hobby so enthusiastically that it starts eating into working hours, or on the other leaves you with little time for your partner and kids, then both work and relationships may start to deteriorate.

So what is it about a hobby that is good for us? The key it seems is whether or not the activity triggers our interest, since interest is accompanied by positive emotions similar to enjoyment and surprise. These feelings often cause us to explore further, adopt new behaviors or pick up new knowledge, which in turn increases our curiosity. So experiencing these positive emotions builds enduring personal resources in a virtuous cycle, creating a true win/win situation.

Suggested hobbies to improve your happiness

- Watercolor painting (it's all in the body movement).

- Making models out of clay (or Play-Doh).

- Gardening (see entry 48).

- Scrapbooking (it's all about keeping happy memories).

- Singing in a choir.

- Doing puzzles.

- Knitting.

- Learning a musical instrument.

- Yoga.

- Starting a fish aquarium.

Visiting an art gallery

☺ # 3 POINTS

How often do you get to visit an art gallery? Chances are that even if you're an art lover, this is something you reserve for holidays, days off, weekends, or special treats, maybe taking the kids too when they're old enough.

For many people, going to a gallery requires making a special effort, but of course if you live or work in a city, you're more likely to have a visual arts venue of some description closer at hand. Research suggests that visiting an art gallery, even for a brief lunchtime trip of about 40 minutes, can significantly reduce the level of the stress hormone cortisol in your body, as well as self-reported levels of stress and arousal.

In a London study, participants reported a 45 percent reduction in their perceived stress levels. What is also interesting is that the drop in cortisol levels was not only very substantial (about 32 percent) but also very quick. Immediately following the gallery visit, stress hormone levels had fallen to below the average for the time of day, whereas under normal circumstances it would take about five hours for them to fall to this level.

So next time you're having a demanding day, think about popping along to your local art gallery for a cup of decaf and a de-stress at lunch time, or even on the way home. Whether you want to gaze at the Gainsboroughs, peruse the Pollocks or marvel at the Monets, it'll do you good.

Making music

2 POINTS ☺

Music is a powerful mood modifier, capable of generating intense emotions, both positive and negative. Music has the capacity to lift our spirits and our energy levels when we're feeling down, as well as induce solemnity, excitement, passion, tranquility, and awe as the occasion demands. Many of us have some kind of relationship with music even if we're not accomplished performers ourselves. We may sing in the bath, tap our fingers to a beat, or hum along to the radio in the car, or, as is so common these days, plug ourselves into an iPod as we commence the long commute.

Music features largely at important life events, singing Happy Birthday for example, or playing the wedding march at a marriage ceremony. Music is also intensely individual; there seems to be something out there for every taste, whether it's reggae, country, metal, jazz, or a subset or fusion of them. It has such a significant cultural impact that young people in the West in particular use music as a means of finding their identity. How important was music in the making or breaking of your first relationships? And how much of the music you listen to now is rooted in the type of music you listened to then?

We know intuitively that music plays a tremendously important role in how we feel and behave from day to day, and science confirms this. Studies have shown that participating in music, for example singing in a choir, can lead to significant feelings of joy, elation, excitement, positive feelings about life as well as loss of the sense of self. In addition, participation in a musical performance leads to greater physical well-being, sociability, and a positive outlook.

Playing

☺ # 2 POINTS

Think back to when you were a child. What was the game you most liked to play? Perhaps tag or hide and seek? Play is the favorite activity among young animals and of course humans—you just have to watch a kitten chasing a piece of string, a puppy with a stick in the park, or a child with a pile of wooden blocks. For most kids, playing is what life is really all about, at least until they go to school! So what is play for? Does it have a function apart from just being a fun way to spend your time?

Scientists have suggested that play is not just about enjoyment, although that's a very important part of it. Play is essential to the successful development of the species, whether non-human or human. Play provides the young with a relatively risk-free opportunity to learn about the world and experiment with new behaviors. It's a way of developing social competence before it really begins to matter.

Thus play is both non-serious and functional, and, some scientists suggest, adaptive: play-fighting for example is a way of practicing real-life hunting skills, which would have ensured the survival of the species thousands of years ago.

Playing brings a great many benefits both in the short and long term. It's fun, it's risk-free, it allows you to be creative and break out of your normal boundaries, it reduces stress, and it gives you the opportunity to develop new skills. Whether you're 6 or 106, playing is most definitely good for you.

53

Binge drinking

5 POINTS ☹

Many of us enjoy an alcoholic drink every now and then but in some countries binge drinking is on the increase. Regular binge drinking doesn't just damage your wallet, it can have many negative effects for your well-being, including stomach ulcers, liver damage, impaired memory, reactions, and judgment, as well as leading to the inevitable hangover and even the risk of potentially fatal alcohol poisoning.

Moderate drinking, on the other hand, is widely thought to be beneficial to your health and happiness. Studies consistently show that drinking one unit a day, especially of red wine, is linked to better physical health, while as far as psychological health goes, there is a known association between alcohol and depression, which is often described as "J shaped," meaning that people who drink moderate amounts of alcohol have lower rates of depression and anxiety disorders than those who are teetotalers, while those who drink excessive amounts have the highest rates of all. So the best advice for the sake of your physical health and happiness is drink only in moderation!

How to drink safely

- Use soft drink or water spacers to pace yourself.

- Drink plenty of water, especially before you go to bed.

- Eat before you drink; food will soak up the alcohol.

- Don't mix your drinks.

- Stick to the recommended limits—try not to exceed more than one or two alcoholic beverages daily.

- Don't drink and drive.

Smiling

☺ # 4 POINTS

How often do you smile every day? Probably not as often as you did as a child, since it's well known that kids smile and laugh more frequently than adults (see entry 58). But you needn't wait for something good to happen before you smile; recent research has proven what Darwin suggested as far back as the 1870s, that whether you're furrowing your brow or giving a big grin, showing your emotions physically intensifies them—so smiling can actually increase your well-being.

In quirky experiments involving holding a pencil in the mouth to either simulate a smile or a frown, scientists have shown that a genuine smile does indeed contribute to feeling happier. It's what's known as "facial feedback." So if you physically mimic a smile or a frown (or indeed any other emotion, using your face or body posture generally), your brain can be tricked into believing that you're actually feeling this particular emotion, with the result that you then feel it for real.

But it's no good smiling half-heartedly. Your smile needs to be genuine (or what scientists call "Duchenne"), one in which the lips are drawn back, the cheeks are raised and wrinkles appear around the eyes. Take a good look at people smiling, and see if you can notice the difference between the real McCoy and a fake one.

In case you find it a bit tricky to generate a genuine grin without prompting, why not keep a few funny photos in your wallet or on your desk to get you started, or get a book of jokes to keep in the office for whenever you feel in need of an instant pick-me-up.

Insomnia

4 POINTS ☹

As those of you who suffer from insomnia know, the more you try to fall asleep the worse it tends to get. Sleep disorders are usually a symptom of an underlying issue, for example depression or stress, which is why taking sleeping pills is often ineffective in the longer term. Research has consistently shown that people who suffer from insomnia experience lower feelings of both psychological and subjective well-being, although the causal direction of this relationship isn't known.

People who sleep an average of six to eight and a half hours per night report the best levels of psychological and subjective well-being. They report fewer symptoms of depression and anxiety, more positive relations with others, plus greater levels of control and purpose in their lives.

The causes of insomnia are well-established, for example, coffee, smoking or taking drugs, stress, depression and anxiety as well as factors such as the bedroom being too hot or too noisy. Luckily the things that you can do to improve your chances of having a good night's sleep are also well researched (see box).

How to improve your sleep

- Establish a winding-down routine.

- When lying in bed, don't focus on what went wrong during the day.

- Avoid caffeinated drinks.

- Don't eat too close to bedtime.

- Exercise regularly.

- Don't clock-watch.

- Go to bed and get up at the same time every day, including weekends.

Keeping a diary

☺

5 POINTS

The process of writing has long been believed to be a cathartic experience, although the scientific evidence to support this has been mixed. If you write about an unpleasant or traumatic event or experience in a structured way (organizing and integrating what happened) then evidence suggests that in the longer term this activity can be beneficial. Not only can it help you find the necessary insight to overcome the painful emotions or thoughts associated with the experience, it can also improve your physical health and enable you to regain a sense of well-being.

Be careful to write about upsetting experiences in a more free-form way, because it's possible that you might get stuck in a cycle of dwelling on what went wrong, without acquiring the perception needed to move on. In this case writing about an unhappy life event may not be liberating at all, and may in fact increase negative mood.

In terms of happy life events, rather than write it all down, it's more important that you replay repetitively what happened in your mind, reliving and savoring the moment without trying to determine its causes or meanings. By taking time to really appreciate the occasion in this way you'll maintain or increase the positive emotion associated with the happy life event.

Long-term benefits of keeping a diary

- Enhanced immune functioning.

- Less fatigue and tension.

- Improved performance at work or school.

- Improved health for asthma and rheumatoid arthritis sufferers.

- Fewer visits to the doctor.

Savoring
5 POINTS ☺

Do you ever get the feeling that time is speeding up, that there are fewer hours in the day than there used to be? Maybe you're rushing from home to work and back again, trying to squeeze in time for the family and those many household chores, as well as some time for your friends and yourself. If this all sounds very familiar to you, you might be wondering whether it's possible to slow down. Well in a sense it is, through the process of savoring.

Savoring, in Positive Psychology terminology, is a bit more than merely relishing or basking in the moment, it's about really noticing, appreciating, and enhancing the positive experiences in your life. By savoring you slow down intentionally, consciously pay attention to all your senses (touch, taste, sight, sound, smell). You stretch out the experience, and concentrate on noticing what it is about the experience that you enjoy, whether it's as simple as sipping a glass of wine, stroking the cat, or musing over the time you scored a hat-trick for the school hockey team.

You can savor in many different ways, for example anticipating the future, appreciating the present moment or reminiscing about the past. Depending on the type of activity chosen, you can engage physically (e.g. luxuriating in a warm bubble bath) or mentally (e.g. reliving a successful moment at work or school). Don't put too much thought into the process though, since analyzing a positive experience can actually make it less enjoyable.

So perhaps it is possible to put some of your hard-earned leisure time to good use, to start savoring the moment rather than rushing to complete the next task. Savoring helps you appreciate your everyday life more, makes time appear to slow down, and boosts your happiness into the bargain. What could be better than that?

Laughter

☺ **4 POINTS**

According to Dr. Madan Kataria, a physician from Mumbai, India, children laugh on average 300 times a day, but by adulthood this has dropped to an average of 7–15 times a day. Yet laughter has so many benefits on our physical and mental fitness that it makes good sense to incorporate more of it into our daily routine.

How laughter improves your happiness

- Acts as a coping mechanism which reduces depression and stress.

- Relieves hay fever symptoms, decreases pain, and allows us to tolerate discomfort more easily.

- Helps protect against illness by increasing T-cells that attack and kill tumor cells and viruses.

- Aids healing after operations and illnesses by stimulating our immune system.

- Reduces blood sugar levels, which aids glucose tolerance for both diabetics and non-diabetics.

- Increases positive emotions, which in turn can boost our creativity.

- Sharpens up our problem-solving skills.

- Releases tension, and can thus make unpleasant experiences more bearable.

- Brings people together—there's nothing better than sharing a joke with a friend and making people laugh.

- May help to prevent heart attacks. Researchers have shown that watching a comedy video can make the blood vessels expand, step up the blood flow by 22 percent, and leave viewers feeling great. Conversely, watching a stressful film can cause a potentially unhealthy narrowing of the arteries, after which blood flow falls by 35 percent.

59

Recreational drugs

5 POINTS ☹

So-called recreational drugs such as cannabis and ecstasy are widely used across the world. According to the United Nations 2007 World Drug Report, the market for cannabis is the largest illicit drug market in the world, with approximately 160 million users.

Some people believe that cannabis is a relatively harmless "soft" drug which they can use regularly without any long-term effects. Also, it is widely claimed that cannabis can be beneficial for sufferers of various medical conditions including cancer, HIV, and multiple sclerosis. Evidence is mounting, however, that cannabis can cause serious psychotic effects, such as paranoia, in regular users.

As well as possible psychological illnesses, we also have to take into account the damage to physical health, for instance to the lungs, if cannabis is smoked. Many people also agree that using cannabis is the equivalent of one foot on the slippery slope to hard drugs such as cocaine and heroin.

That transition can lead to all sorts of additional problems, such as the increased likelihood of getting into debt or crime in order to fund your drug habit. Both cocaine and heroin are highly addictive—you end up having to take more and more to get the same high. And that's without mentioning the unpleasant side effects and the possibility of feeling paranoid and depressed. Do recreational drugs improve your well-being? Well, in the very short term (and we're talking as little as 30 minutes here) some might argue the answer has to be yes. But the risks are enormous, and in the long-term, once addicted, the answer is a definite no!

Unless you live as a complete hermit, your relationships with other people contribute significantly to how you feel every day, so we ve devoted a chapter to look at just that.

Even the briefest of encounters with acquaintances or complete strangers are opportunities to boost your happiness, and theirs. We re not talking grand gestures here, just taking the time to smile, say hello, be polite, and be helpful.

What really matters to our happiness is the quality of our relationships with others, not the number. In reality you don t need a huge circle of friends around you a small group of close friends, people you can trust and rely on for help and support in bad times, and who you want to share your successes with in the good, is a far more important contributor to your well-being. Having these close friendships in person is also more important to your happiness than having tens or hundreds of remote people who you can chat to online. And don t forget that sometimes people we think of as friends may subconsciously be doing us more harm than good. If you tend to feel worse rather than better after seeing a so-called friend, it s time to consider ending that relationship.

So spend some time thinking about the important relationships you have, how they add to your overall well-being, and ways in which you can improve them further. In terms of increasing your happiness, time spent doing this will be a very good investment.

PART FOUR

Relationships

Love

☺ # 5 POINTS

"Scientists discover link between love and happiness!" Not much of a headline is it? It's something we seem to have always known. Not only that but the most fundamental aspects of love, whether passionate, obsessive, romantic, platonic, or unrequited, transcend both time and place—whether you go back thousands of years to explore early Greek and Roman mythology or browse the fiction section of your local bookshop.

But love is a double-edged sword, as you will also know if you've ever experienced unrequited love or been dumped or divorced by a partner. At these times, love brings anything but happiness.

Essentially though, human beings are social animals—the future of the human race is dependent on us finding a mate we can love and live with. We are then able to reproduce and bring up our children in a loving and protected environment so that they too can be happy and successful in love. According to researchers Baumeister and Leary, humans are a group species with a fundamental need to belong. So it's not surprising that in studies, people in a relationship are happier than those who are not. But unfortunately what we don't know is whether people who are satisfied with their romantic partner are happier, or whether people who are happier are more satisfied with their relationships.

Widowhood

5 POINTS ☹

Although every individual's response to bereavement varies considerably, it isn't surprising that the average married person reports significantly less life satisfaction in the years after being widowed than in the year prior to being widowed. Over time, people adapt to the loss of their spouse; having hit rock bottom their satisfaction with life starts to increase again. But if they don't remarry, they don't necessarily return to their original levels of satisfaction.

Research indicates that bereaved individuals who display positive emotions, genuine laughs, and smiles up to six months after the death of their spouse exhibit better adjustment, increased enjoyment, and better social relations. This doesn't mean that these people who don't show the traditional signs of grieving are heartless or indifferent, rather that they are capable of genuine resilience. The reverse is also true: bereaved people who show negative emotions, and in particular anger, also showed more grief at 14 months and poorer perceived health through 25 months.

The culture of the society also makes a difference to the well-being of the bereaved. Widows and widowers fare relatively better in collectivist cultures than they do in individualistic ones, which is probably because there is greater social support in collectivist cultures.

Good sex

☺ **5 POINTS**

There's no doubt that sex is a much less private affair than it used to be even 30 or 40 years ago. The commercialization of sex is evident everywhere, from the sale of cars and clothes to tooth-whitening kits and detergents. If money makes the world go round, sex can't be far behind! It's relatively recently, with the arrival of the world's first test tube baby in 1978, that sex and the survival of the human race have really become separated—until then the only way to procreate was through sex, so no wonder we have evolved over the preceding millennia to find it a pleasurable experience.

Physical health is an important part of overall mental well-being (see entry 45), and sex is good for our physical health in a number of ways: it improves our respiratory, immune, circulatory, and cardiovascular systems, as well as developing strength, muscle tone, and flexibility.

Sex also has a positive impact on our emotional well-being, and research has shown that it's not having a large number of sexual partners that is more satisfying but that both men and women are happier when they'd had only one partner in the past 12 months and were also married to them.

We know that sex makes us feel good, certainly in the short term, but does it directly benefit our psychological well-being and contribute to our level of happiness and life satisfaction over a longer period of time? Do we naturally become repressed or frustrated and therefore unhappy without it?

For many people, having a satisfying sex life seems to be a fundamental part of what it means to be happy, but there is evidence that for some people, sex isn't actually such a big deal. If they're in a relationship, providing they're matched with a partner who feels the same, infrequent sex will not cause any problem for their relationship or their emotional well-being. And many people make celibacy a life choice, and manage perfectly happily without sex at all.

How can sex make you happy?

Studies suggest that sex is an important part of creating and maintaining positive human relationships because it fulfils three basic psychological needs:

1. Being intimate, loved, desired, and respected satisfies the need to feel close to other people.

2. When both partners can talk to each other openly about their sexual desires and agree on what they do in bed, their need to feel that their activities are self-chosen and self-endorsed is fulfilled.

3. For all its apparent mystery, sex is a skill like any other; the more you practice the better you get, thus fulfilling the need to feel competent.

Successful marriage

☺ **5 POINTS**

It's been long established in the psychology world that having close and loving relationships and feeling secure and attached to other people are fundamental human needs, contributing not only to the successful development of children into adults, but also to the survival of the human race. We know that types of marriage vary across the globe. In some societies the only legally permissible form is between one man and one woman; in others, same sex unions or those where a person has more than one spouse are perfectly legal. One of the most reliable findings from numerous studies of relationships and happiness is that peope who are married are happier than those who aren't.

Happiness levels for married and unmarried people

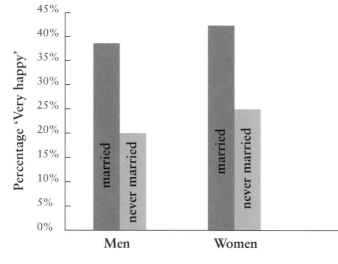

For the romantics among you, this may well confirm what you always believed, that traditional relationships that lead to marriage are the best ones. At the same time however, this evidence doesn't prove that getting married will make you happier; it may be that being married makes you happier, or it may be that happy people are more likely to get married in the first place.

One study found that middle-aged women whose college yearbook photographs some 30 years earlier showed them smiling in a genuine way (what psychologists call a "Duchenne smile," see entry 54), had more satisfying and long-standing marriages than those women whose yearbook smiles were false. The attractiveness of the women was also rated, but this was not related to the happiness of their marriage. This suggests that more happy people do indeed form more happy marriages.

British psychologist Daniel Nettle quotes a large German study that also supports the view that on the whole, happy people are more likely to get married than unhappy people. This research indicated that getting married increases the individual's happiness set point (see How to Use this Book on p8) regardless of where they started. The bad news is that this boost to happiness doesn't last forever, and eventually tails off. However, the good news is that even after many years, those people who initially responded to marriage with a big increase in happiness retained enough to be happier than when they started out. So maybe there is some truth in fairytale "happily ever after" endings after all.

Cohabiting

☺ **3 POINTS**

Although the number of adults who choose to live together rather than marry varies widely from country to country, co-habiting has increased dramatically in industrialized countries over the past 40 or 50 years.

In America the 2000 census indicates that 5.5 million couples were living together but not married, up from 3.2 million in 1990 and 439,000 in 1960. In Australia between 1996 and 2001, the number of adults living together rose by 28 percent from 744,100 to 951,500. In the UK the proportion rose from 11 percent in 1979 to 29 percent in 1998.

For many couples, cohabitation is an alternative to marriage, for others it's usually a precursor to marriage. The increasing number of people who live together suggests that it must be making them happy—why else would they do it?

The happiness of cohabiting couples seems to depend on what kind of culture they live in. In countries with collectivist cultures unmarried people living together report lower life satisfaction and more negative emotions than married or single individuals. One reason for this could be that collectivist societies are more traditional and therefore less accepting of living together before marriage. In individualist cultures, such as the US, the UK, and Western Europe, cohabiting couples are happier and more satisfied with their lives than either married or single people.

Overall, data does confirm that cohabiting people are happier on the whole than the single, divorced, or widowed. Generally, however, they are not as happy as married couples, and they're more likely to suffer from depression than either the married, the never married, or people who have divorced once.

Divorce

4 POINTS ☹

Getting divorced is the second most stressful life event after the death of one's spouse; generally speaking, divorce is even more stressful than losing your job or the death of another family member. Not surprisingly then, it can have a significant and long lasting negative effect on both your physical health and your happiness.

The state of your physical health can have an effect on your emotional health (see entries 4 and 45), and research indicates that the divorced visit their doctor more frequently than people who are married, single, or widowed. Separation and divorce also contribute to an increased risk of alcohol abuse which can have a detrimental effect on your happiness (see entry 53): in one study of chronic problem drinkers, the separated and divorced accounted for 70 percent, whereas the married accounted for 15 percent.

In relation to psychological health, divorce is associated with increased anxiety and depression; as a result divorced people are more likely to be admitted to a psychiatric hospital, or to commit suicide than single or married people. The lack of interpersonal closeness, particularly for divorced men, contributes to the fall in happiness and the increase in stress levels.

Divorce is not always a bad thing; there is evidence that staying unhappily married is associated with significantly lower levels of overall happiness, life satisfaction, self-esteem, and health along with elevated levels of psychological distress. So it's better for one's long-term health and happiness to divorce than to stay in an unhappy marriage. And the opportunity to marry again seems to diminish, if not totally eliminate, the unhappiness associated with divorce.

Being single

☹ # 1 POINT

Being young, free, and single is often portrayed in the popular media as a highly desirable status, especially for men—you can have relationships (either consecutively or simultaneously) with lots of people but not have any of the responsibility. Portrayals of female singletons, however, tend to be a different story—who can forget the hapless Bridget Jones searching for Mr. Right while charting the cigarettes and the booze in her diary? Being married is also frequently clichéd in different ways; it's either heaven and the answer to all your dreams or it's hell—the equivalent of wearing a ball and chain around your leg—you don't do it unless you've got no other alternative.

Life as a singleton might be fun for a time, but the independence and lack of restrictions are not without their downside. Human beings need other people to survive, not just for procreation but for the psychological support that you get from living with others.

Numerous studies indicate that single people (i.e. those who have never married) are significantly less happy than those who are married, although as mentioned in entry 63, this could be because they tend to be more miserable, and thus less likely to get married in the first place. If you're single and unhappy, getting married is unlikely to make you happier in the long term. You'd be better off postponing wedding plans until you've tackled the underlying issues of your unhappiness.

Unhappily married

4 POINTS ☹

Getting married has the potential to raise your happiness set point permanently (see entry 63). But before you rush off to book the church, bear in mind that it's not a simple case of marriage = happiness, although this is often what gets portrayed in romantic fiction. In reality it's a little more complicated than that.

Studies show that getting married can potentially make you happier. However, according to psychologist David Myers, being unhappily married is worse for you than being single or divorced. What's more, the state of your marriage affects how satisfied you are with life in general: only 3 percent of those in a "not too happy" marriage were very satisfied with their lives as a whole, compared to 10 percent of people in "pretty happy" marriages and 57 percent in "very happy" marriages.

It's sometimes said that "men marry for better and women for worse," suggesting that marriage increases men's happiness more than it does women's. Although there is some indication that wives get more depressed in a bad marriage, research shows that single women aren't actually happier than married ones.

So what contributes to a satisfying and long lasting marriage? Physical attractiveness, sexual compatibility, and similar attitudes, interests, and values are all important. In addition, happy couples create a "bank account" of positive feelings about their partner and their marriage which they can draw on especially during times of conflict.

Close friends

☺ **5 POINTS**

The quality of our relationships with others can have a significant impact on our general wellbeing, and having close friends in whom we can confide is a very important source of happiness. In one study carried out on 222 college students it was found that the key difference between the happiest 10 percent of the group and the rest of them was that the former had rich and satisfying interpersonal lives. They also spent the least time alone and the most time socializing, and were rated highest on good relationships by themselves and by others.

The number of close friends people have typically seems to be pretty small, possibly because in practical terms most of us don't have the time and energy needed to maintain and keep in contact with a large number of close relationships. However, having a smaller number of intimate friends who you can trust and

confide in is also more beneficial to your happiness, rather than having a larger group of more casual acquaintances.

It's also often the case that while people continue to make new friends over the course of their lives, and lose contact with old, often the same close friends are kept throughout one's life. What does seem to change is the amount of time people spend with their friends. Studies have shown that adolescents spend approximately 30 percent of their time with friends, whereas adults spend less than 10 percent.

And what about best friends? These are the friends who bring out the best in us, who we can depend on come what may, and who are kind, loving, honest, and loyal to us. Research shows that these qualities are far more important in explaining a best friendship than features like the friend's accomplishments, attractiveness, or status. So be sure to make time for the friendships in your life.

How friendships can make you happy

- Feeling that you belong somewhere is a fundamental human need, and having friends who accept us, fulfills this need.

- Friendship provides social support—we do each other favors, and we always know that there is someone to lean on in times of need.

- Happy people make more desirable friends than unhappy people, so therefore they're more often selected as companions by others.

Acts of kindness

☺ **5 POINTS**

How often do you go out of your way to help someone else, a friend, colleague, or even a stranger? Take a few minutes to think about it. Maybe you ran an errand for your elderly neighbor, helped a busy mom carry her stroller up some steps, or donated blood?

Doing good deeds often not only boosts your mood temporarily, it also leads to long lasting happiness, as well as making other people feel good too. So it's a brilliant win-win activity, plus it doesn't have to cost you anything.

What scientific studies also show is that acts of kindness have more impact on your well-being if you do a variety of different things, rather than repeating the same activity a number of times.

Why kind acts make you happier

Researchers suggest a number of reasons why doing kind acts for others make you happier:

- They may make you feel more confident, in control, and optimistic about your ability to make a difference.

- They enable you to connect with other people (a basic human need), which contributes to your happiness.

- They may make you feel more positive about other people and the community you live in, and foster cooperation between people.

Going to church

2 POINTS ☺

Religious and spiritual people tend to be happier than those who aren't. As well as a more well-defined system of beliefs and values, higher levels of hope and optimism, and better coping styles, it's been suggested that the social and emotional support provided by faith communities also contributes to greater well-being. In studies, the frequency with which members of faith communities attend their church, temple, or other religious setting has been found to be significantly connected to happiness, indicating that the support that people get from relationships does indeed have a very positive impact on wellbeing.

Religious groups are often fairly homogenous, so members may feel that their beliefs, values, and life choices are constantly being affirmed, leading to improved self-esteem and confidence. But it's not just the people who receive social and emotional support from their religious community who benefit; research also indicates that volunteering and helping others in a religious setting benefits the providers of the support as much as it does the recipients (see entry 69).

Family fights

☹ # 1 POINT

There's an old saying, "you can choose your friends, but you can't choose your family." If you have brothers and sisters the chances are that you quarrelled when you were kids. Perhaps you borrowed each other's toys or clothes without asking, got each other into trouble with your parents, or fell out over which TV channel to watch. And as for arguing with your mom and dad, well, even if you are as good as gold when you're a child, once you become a teenager conflict with parents is almost inevitable. It's part of normal growing up and finding your independence.

Interestingly, research shows that adolescents argue more with their mothers than they do with their fathers or siblings. One reason for this might be that children typically have a much closer relationship with their mother, thus the process of growing up and becoming independent of her is likely to be more problematic and therefore result in more conflict.

It shouldn't be surprising to find that family differences turn out to have an impact on teenagers' wellbeing; resolving conflicts with parents is linked to greater well-being when measured in terms of self-esteem, depression, and risky behavior (taking drugs, drinking, etc.). In particular, because arguments with mothers tend to be of a personal nature, such as choice of friends and appearance, it's easy to see why these types of conflicts would have an impact on self-esteem. Of course, what we don't know is whether failing to resolve conflicts causes lower well-being, or whether adolescents with lower well-being are less likely to resolve the conflicts they have. Either way, it makes sense for parents to try and ensure that any family fights are settled constructively.

Broken home
1 POINT

There's growing scientific evidence that the happiness of children whose parents divorce or who have single mothers is negatively affected in several ways compared to children brought up by both biological parents. This is the case regardless of the child's age or race/ethnicity. What's even more astonishing is that these effects don't disappear even when the parents subsequently marry or remarry.

Economist Richard Layard puts forward four reasons why living with a single parent is bad for a child's happiness: 1) typically family income is substantially reduced: for example, 49 percent of lone parent households in the UK are income poor, compared with 24 percent of single people without children, 2) there is less input and guidance from the parent who leaves, 3) often the family moves to a new area, leaving old friends behind, and 4) the child can feel betrayed, so even if they see the absent parent regularly, it can still harm their relationship.

A study of seven-year olds found that children whose parents separated were almost twice as likely to suffer from depression compared with children whose parents stayed together, and adolescents are twice as likely to have a criminal conviction at the age of 15 and leave high school without a diploma if their biological parents are living apart.

Of course children can be extremely resilient, and as adults it is possible for them to remedy any issues they had growing up with divorced parents or in a single-parent family, and negate any negative effects this had on their happiness as children.

Owning a pet

☺ **2 POINTS**

It's well established that pet ownership confers a number of physical health benefits, such as reducing blood pressure, heart rate, stress, and depression. But there may also be mental benefits; studies indicate that assistance dogs such as guide dogs for the blind have a positive influence on the self-esteem and well-being of people with disabilities. Owning a dog has more beneficial effects on our physical and mental health than owning a cat, although the reasons for this are not yet entirely clear. Dr Deborah Wells of Queen's University, Belfast suggests that dogs can aid our health by preventing minor ailments such as colds and headaches, facilitating recovery from illness, and helping to predict certain ailments, such as epileptic seizures.

Cats can be good for you too—in one study, participants, who were either cat or dog owners or not, were required to complete mental arithmetic tests, and put their hand in a bucket of icy water for two minutes. Pet owners who did the tests in the presence of their pets exhibited significantly lower heart rate and blood pressure, and recovered faster afterwards, than did the non-owners.

It's likely that promenading in the local park brings you into contact with other dog owners, thus fulfilling the fundamental human need of connecting with other people. Research may not yet give us all the answers, but owning and caring for a much-loved pet can do wonders for your physical health and may do the same for your happiness.

74

Conflict at work
1 POINT ☹

How often do you experience interpersonal problems in the workplace? Unless you work alone and/or from home, it's likely that the problems that cause you the most grief at work are of an interpersonal rather than technical nature. Strange as it might seem, although common sense tells us that interpersonal conflict is likely to be at the root of most occupational stress and the cause of reduced happiness and job satisfaction, it's only recently that it has been studied scientifically.

In the business world, conflict at work is such an important subject that most large employers have formal grievance and discipline procedures in place. Nevertheless there are many occasions when embarking on a formal process to resolve conflict would seem heavy-handed.

Conflict can crop up between individuals at work for all sorts of reasons, such as having different ideas as to how a task needs to be done, or differences over personal beliefs and values. Research indicates that only the latter types of problems, those based on interpersonal relationships, cause conflict stress, i.e., they trigger feelings of reduced control and undermine one's sense of self, resulting in tension, anxiety, stress, and reduced well-being. When people are in conflict they also tend to find it more difficult to communicate, making it difficult to find the high quality information needed to find a resolution. What often happens as a result is that the conflict intensifies, creating a negative downward spiral.

Not all employees are adversely affected by relationship conflict at work, since individual personality characteristics lead to different interpretations and reactions. Since we often don't know how people will react to stress until it's too late, many big employers train their managers in mediation skills that can prevent the occurrence of a conflict that can only be resolved through formal procedures.

Emotional intelligence

☺ ## 1 POINT

When you're feeling sad, how good are you at turning your mood around? Do you find ways to manage your sadness so that it doesn't seriously impact on other areas of your life, or do you wallow in it? Emotional intelligence (EQ) is the capacity to recognize and manage our emotions and those of others close to us. If we can identify emotional messages in the expression and tone of others, we're more likely to understand their perspective and empathize; by understanding how emotions affect our thinking, we can use them for more effective problem solving, decision making, and creative pursuits. And managing our emotions effectively—improving a bad mood, relaxing when nervous, or remaining calm when angry, is the crux of emotional intelligence and can increase our chances of happiness.

How to manage your emotions

- Expend some energy—get some physical exercise.

- Give yourself a pep-talk—or find a friend to give you one.

- Change position—get up from your desk, look up, stretch and walk around.

- Go outside if you can.

- Don't resort to drink, drugs, or comfort food.

- Listen to some relaxing music.

- Don't avoid the person or thing that has upset you.

- Go to a yoga class.

- Meditate.

- Find a pleasant distraction—spend an hour on your favorite hobby, or run an errand for someone.

- Find a friend to chat with.

Sharing good news
1 POINT ☺

Wellbeing isn't always about how you react to negative events and manage when things go wrong (although this is important); it's also about what you do when things go right. For example, what do you tend to do when you have a piece of good news? Say you get promoted, win $100 in the lottery, or get some exceptional feedback about a project you've just finished—do you share it with other people right away or not?

Back in 1994 scientists ran tests to show that when you share good news with others or celebrate the event, you experience additional happiness over and above the happiness associated with the event itself, possibly because in retelling the event, you re-experience it. Sharing or celebrating good news means you get the best of both worlds. What's more, the more people you tell, the more your happiness increases. Researchers have also suggested that sharing or celebrating good news with other people strengthens social relationships and builds trust and self-esteem.

The response you get from the people you share the news with is crucial. If they react enthusiastically, openly showing that they're pleased for you by talking positively about your success, your well-being will be enhanced. On the other hand, if they react negatively, either by actively scoffing at your success, or by ignoring it, your sense of well-being is likely to be reduced.

So next time you have a piece of good news, make sure you share it with as many of your friends as possible. And when someone shares their good news with you, be genuinely pleased for them; you'll be making them happier in the process.

According to Professor Martin Seligman, former President of the American Psychological Association and founder of the Positive Psychology movement, human happiness is not just about pleasure, engagement, and good relationships; it s also about positive achievement and meaning. In this chapter we focus on these two categories, which we call fulfillment, and cover subjects as broad as having children, your work, and being religious or spiritual.

It s not easy to say how crucial fulfillment is overall since depends on each individual. It s possible to take a moral perspective and suggest that some types of happiness are more worthy than others, but we re not interested in following that line of argument here. For some people, earthly pleasures will be far more important to their happiness than finding meaning or purpose in their lives, and who are we to tell them otherwise? Where science can help is by indicating if certain types of activities are likely to lead to longer lasting happiness. By and large, the more hedonistic happiness associated with physical activities like eating, drinking, or shopping bring short-term pleasure, but can work against your happiness in the long-term. So the factors in this chapter concentrate on the things you can do and choices you can make to achieve enduring happiness.

PART FIVE

Fulfillment

Goals

☺ # 5 POINTS

Some psychologists suggest that the ability to reflect, to choose a direction in life, and to be motivated to pursue certain goals are also key components of psychological well-being. The crucial thing in having a goal is not what the goal is or even whether it's actually achieved, but whether the action of pursuing it helps you meet your basic psychological needs (see below).

Engaging in activities that are intrinsically motivating leads to greater satisfaction and better physical and psychological well-being. In one study in a nursing home, one group of residents was given the freedom to make choices and the responsibility of caring for a plant, while another group had decisions made for them and the plant was looked after by staff. The residents in the first group were more active and had a higher well-being than those in the second group. Other studies of weight loss or alcohol treatment programs also show that people who are motivated to pursue their goals are more likely to succeed, and less likely to relapse.

How having a goal increases happiness

Having a goal fulfills basic psychological needs that are crucial for happiness:

1. Autonomy: being free to choose what you want to do.

2. Competence: feeling effective.

3. Pleasure-stimulation: sense of having fun.

4. Physical health.

5. Security: having a sense of order in life.

6. Self-esteem: feeling worthy.

7. Self-actualization: a sense that you are growing toward an ideal self or world.

8. Relatedness: feeling connected to others

Education

1 POINT ☺

Although empirical research has discovered that IQ and happiness aren't linked, it has shown that there is a small correlation between education and happiness, particularly for people in underdeveloped countries, or for low-income groups in developed countries.

One reason for this could be that education confers disproportionate benefits on people in poor countries. In other words, if you live in an underdeveloped country and you don't have an education, you may find it difficult to satisfy the basic physical needs of finding food and shelter. You stand a much better chance if you're educated. The benefits of education could also be due to the relationship that it has with occupational status and income; if you're very poor, earning more money (which would be more likely if you're more educated and have a better job) does bring greater happiness. It's just that this is only true up to a point, after which the increases in happiness start to level out.

In developed countries, where the majority of poor people already have their basic needs met, education is often seen as a means to greater individual freedom and empowerment. And making progress towards desired goals (whatever they may be) has also been shown to lead to great levels of psychological well-being.

$$1+1=2 \qquad 1+6=7$$
$$1+2=3 \qquad 1+7=8$$
$$1+3=4 \qquad 1+8=9$$
$$1+4=5 \qquad 1+9=10$$
$$1+5=6 \qquad 1+10=11$$

Getting things done

☺ ## 2 POINTS

Psychologists have found that it is not so much the completion of a goal that matters, but the progress you make towards it (see entry 77). And the key to making progress with "big" goals is to break them down into small steps so that they are manageable.

In one study, three groups of people were given nonsense words to interpret, and received false feedback on their performance: the first group was told they were getting about 50 percent of the answers correct. The second group was told they'd decreased from getting almost all correct to getting 50 percent correct. The third group were told they'd gone from getting very few correct to getting 50 percent correct. The third group—i.e., the people who showed the greatest improvement on the task—were the ones who felt the happiest, even though in absolute terms they did not get a higher number of correct answers.

How to get things done

- If you are stuck on a particular goal and seem unable to make any headway, try to break it down into smaller steps.

- Review your progress frequently—constantly ask yourself what you could do differently.

- Don't be afraid to ask for help.

- If you can, delegate the task (or parts of it). Ask someone to help you and do the job together.

- Make chores fun by finding new ways to do them. For example, make it into a competition—time yourself doing the weeding or cleaning and see if you can do it quicker next time.

Unemployment
2 POINTS ☹

It's probably no surprise to you that employment status is directly related to happiness; employed people tend to be happier than unemployed people. Even if we don't think of our job as a vocation (see entry 91), generally it is personally meaningful in some way, for instance it gives us independence, status in our community, allows us to take care of our family, or enables us to pursue our favorite leisure time activity. For many people, their job also provides them with social relationships and self-esteem. So losing our job is devastating; not only does your income go down, but you lose all these other intangible benefits too. In fact, scientists who have studied this area suggest that the monetary costs are very small compared with the non-monetary costs.

There's no doubt that being unemployed can make you unhappy, but could there be a possibility that less happy people actually become unemployed more often than happy ones? As yet science has not provided a clear-cut answer.

Research does indicate that we don't get used to being unemployed either (see entry 19). Unlike other misfortunes, it seems that we don't bounce back to our happiness set point very easily with regards to employment. A large scale European study in the 1990s showed that long-term unemployment is barely different than shorter duration, so it feels just as bad after a year as it does in the first month. And if this isn't bad enough, there's evidence that the experience of being unemployed in the past can continue to haunt you, even once you find a job again, by reducing your current well-being.

Self-esteem

☺ # 2 POINTS

Self-esteem is generally high in childhood, then takes a battering during adolescence, gradually increasing again in early- to mid-adulthood, before starting to decline as we enter old age. But what is the evidence that low self-esteem is bad or high self-esteem is good? And can having higher self-esteem make you happier?

One international study of over 13,000 students found a significant relationship between self-esteem and happiness. Another separate study of people aged 51 to 95 came to a similar conclusion, and an analysis of 137 different personality traits found that self-esteem again was one of the strongest predictors. So with all this evidence showing how important self-esteem is for happiness, why are some psychologists still very against it?

The problem is that high self-esteem sometimes leads people to conclude that they are doing better than they are, and gives an exaggerated sense of self-importance. People with high but unstable self-esteem can be prone to aggression; on the surface they appear confident and secure, but in reality are highly sensitive. When they feel that their sense of self is being challenged, they can quickly become angry. Some psychologists believe that creating ways to boost self-esteem is therefore problematic, because it focuses the attention inwards (on the rights of the self) instead of outwards (on the rights of society at large).

Lack of self-discipline
2 POINTS ☹

How often is your self-discipline really tested? Perhaps you're trying to give up smoking or trying to stick to a physical exercise regime. Self-discipline functions a bit like a muscle—it needs practice, and the more you exercise it the stronger it gets. With strong self-discipline, you can control your emotions, impulses, and appetites, as well as your performance. What this means in effect is that by using self-control in practical areas of your life such as eating healthily, you can build the necessary discipline to manage how happy (or sad) you feel. Self-discipline is also vital to your overall happiness because many of the activities which boost your happiness (such as regular exercise) will take a while to develop into a habit.

Scientists have demonstrated that self-control can have dramatic benefits in life. For instance, people with high self-control are less likely to turn to drugs, alcohol, and crime, and are more likely to manage their money well and get along better with other people. In a longitudinal study, preschool children who were most successful at delaying gratification were more academically and socially successful as adolescents, as rated by their peers and teachers. Other studies have also shown that of 32 different personality measures, self-discipline was the only one that predicted grade point average.

So how do you go about increasing your self-discipline? You'll need to take small steps at the start and build up from there. The key is to set the bar high enough that you have something to aim for, but not so high that you haven't got a hope of achieving it.

Materialism

☹ **4 POINTS**

Although there has been a significant rise in wealth in the past 50 years in most developed countries, there hasn't been a corresponding increase in wellbeing (see entry 3). In fact levels of happiness have stayed pretty much the same. This might seem surprising when we consider how much higher our standard of living is now. But in the developed world we're constantly bombarded with overt marketing messages urging us to splurge on a new car, dishwasher, or cell phone, or with subconscious ones which we pick up by constantly comparing ourselves with wealthy celebrities whose lives are played out on the screen in our living rooms.

According to psychologist Tim Kasser, the problem occurs because we confuse our wants and needs. He says people who have materialistic values (see entry 98) and who pursue goals such as wealth, possessions, celebrity, and status tend to have lower life satisfaction and self-esteem, place less emphasis on relationships with other people, contribute less to their community, and have lower regard for environmental issues. What hasn't been established is whether materialism causes these psychological issues or vice versa. There's scientific evidence that spending money on experiences, such as going on vacation or taking up a new hobby, makes people happier than spending it on possessions. So rather than going shopping for the latest designer fashions or gadgets, why not consider spending the same money on a vacation to somewhere new?

Appreciating excellence
2 POINTS ☺

Our ability to appreciate excellence, whether in nature or manmade, is considered to be one of the most important strengths according to research carried out in the past decade to identify universal strengths and virtues. A person who is high on this strength not only feels a sense of wonderment at what is going on around them in the natural world—such as noticing the first crocus in spring or the way the sidewalks seem to sparkle with frost in the winter—but also at the gifts and talents shown by people around them, admiring how a potter can turn a shapeless lump of red clay into a beautiful work of art for example, or how a lecturer inspires students with lifelong passion for their subject.

A person who is low on the strength of appreciation is wearing metaphorical blinkers—they might see what is going on around them, but it fails to move them emotionally. Being open to beauty and excellence suggests that you are creating opportunities to feel the positive emotions of joy, pleasure and elation, whereas if you don't even take the time to notice these things, that door is well and truly closed.

It would be reasonable to assume that feeling a sense of deep appreciation must be correlated with greater happiness. In fact the scientific evidence is almost nonexistent, partly because there is no tried-and-true method to measure appreciation at the moment. Once one has been developed, scientists will be able to confirm that appreciating beauty and excellence can make us happier, and by how much.

Job satisfaction

☺

2 POINTS

In a major study of job satisfaction and happiness based on American General Social Survey data, it was found that the majority of American workers are actually pretty satisfied at work. Approximately half said they were very satisfied, with 40 percent moderately satisfied. Data from 50,000 randomly sampled people from 18

Job satisfaction in Europe 1995-1996

Country	very satisfied	moderately satisfied	total satisfied	a little disatisfied	very disatisfied
S Ireland	57	38	95	4	1
Denmark	50	45	95	3	2
Belgium	44	49	93	6	1
Luxembourg	40	53	93	5	2
Finland	31	62	93	6	2
Netherlands	46	46	92	7	1
Sweden	39	53	92	5	2
E Germany	34	56	90	9	2
Austria	44	45	89	9	1
UK	38	49	87	9	5
W Germany	34	51	85	11	4
Portugal	21	62	83	13	3
Italy	26	56	82	15	4
France	22	60	82	14	5
Spain	23	57	80	16	4
Greece	11	50	61	29	9
All	35	52	87	10	3

European Union countries in the late 1990s reveals similar information; that job satisfaction is pretty high with only a small minority saying they are unhappy with their work.

Expectation of job loss appears to have one of the largest negative effects on job satisfaction, and thus on well-being, although there are other factors including increasing stress, responsibility, and effort.

Job satisfaction and well-being have less to do with salary or status of a job, and more to do with how much control you have over the type of work you do every day and how meaningful your job is (see entry 91). Even though the amount of stress you experience day-to-day tends to increase as you rise through the ranks, so too does your autonomy, and it is this, or the lack of it, which affects your well-being and satisfaction at work.

When we look at job satisfaction trends over time, however, we see there is a small but significant shift downwards: in the 1970s 56 percent of Americans over 30 were very satisfied, in the 1980s this had fallen to 52 percent, and in the 1990s to 48 percent. This could be because of raised expectations of employees in developed countries, or because of increased stress caused by constant change. Whether the decline will continue over the long term is anyone's guess, but employers need to be prepared for the worst.

Personal growth

☺ # 3 POINTS

Personal growth is a valuable life goal; continuing to try new things, learn new skills, and further develop yourself as a person can make a difference to your happiness. The reason is that goals related to realizing one's potential are linked to decreased depression, greater life satisfaction, and increased happiness.

From a practical perspective, personal development has also become a big thing in many businesses. Now employees at all levels are encouraged to develop themselves in new areas, acquire new skills, and volunteer for assignments that will strengthen self-confidence and resilience, making it easier for them to take on new roles in the future.

Personal growth and happiness

According to American psychologist Carol Ryff, people who score highly on personal growth:

- Are open to new experiences and activities, and like to try new ways of doing things (see entry 40).

- Think it's important to have experiences which challenge how they think about themselves and the world.

- See themselves as continually growing and expanding.

- See improvement in themselves and their behavior over time.

- Become more effective over time.

- Enjoy being in new situations which mean they have to change their familiar ways of doing things.

Job insecurity
1 POINT ☹

Losing one's job is one of the most stressful life events after bereavement and divorce, and it leads to much lower life satisfaction overall.

In a study of nine countries including the UK and the US, the UK performed consistently badly on participants' perceptions of job security, even when judged against other English-speaking nations. This suggests that job security is not just a factor of the type of job or industry but that there are other factors at play.

Studies in the US, Finland, and Australia show that, not surprisingly, job insecurity is linked to many different measures of well-being, among them lower self-esteem, marital dissatisfaction, anxiety, and depression. Feeling secure at work, on the other hand, leads to increased psychological well-being and greater job satisfaction.

The findings from a study using data from 12 European countries confirm that employees in public sector jobs feel most secure, those in temporary jobs feel least secure, with those in permanent private sector jobs falling somewhere in between. As public sector jobs tend to be most insulated from the impact of economic problems and recession, this is probably not surprising. Just as happiness is "U-shaped" in age, so is the perception of job security; it starts high in young adulthood, reaching a low point in one's 40s, then increases steadily up to retirement. This might be due to practical reasons such as additional family responsibilities that are typically present in middle age. Once the kids have flown the nest, responsibilities decrease, concerns about job insecurity fade, and happiness increases. It will be interesting to see whether the position of the low-point on the U-shaped curve changes as people in the West start their families later, and young people take longer to become financially independent.

Using your strengths

☺ # 5 POINTS

Do you know what your strengths are? If not it's important that you spend some time now thinking about it. The reason is this: studies show that people who use their strengths in new ways every day for one week have higher happiness and lower depression levels for six months after.

So how can you identify your strengths? One option is to complete an online assessment—there are several commercial approaches to using strengths at work, as well as other more universal approaches, such as the VIA Inventory of Strengths. If you don't want to do an online assessment, there are some questions that will help you get more familiar with your forte (see below).

The next step is to find ways of using your strengths. For example, if your strength is curiosity, chose an unfamiliar dish from the restaurant menu instead of your old favorite. If it's leadership, organize a social get-together for your neighbors. If it's creativity, enroll in a painting or pottery class. See how many different ways you can use your strengths and what a difference it makes to your happiness.

How to identify your strengths

- Think about some everyday things that you enjoy doing—what would you say you enjoy the most and why?

- What are you doing when at your best?

- What are you doing when you feel most alive and full of energy?

- Thinking back to when you were young, what were your best times? What were you doing?

- What are you doing when you feel that you are expressing the real you?

Creativity

1 POINT ☺

Research has shown that feeling positive and upbeat increases creativity, whereas negative emotions often stifle it. In studies, groups of participants watched five-minute long video clips that induced either a positive or a neutral mood. Those who watched the comedy clip performed better on tasks which required them to solve a problem creatively than those who watched the neutral clip.

In one recent study, participants suffering from post-traumatic stress were invited to take part in drawing sessions. One group was instructed to draw a large circle on a piece of paper and then fill the circle with any symbols, patterns, or designs that represented the feelings or emotions related to their trauma. Participants in the control group were asked to draw a random object in as much detail as possible. Although the participants in the mandala group had experienced more severe symptoms of trauma than those in the control group, one month after the study their symptoms has significantly decreased. The symptoms of the participants in the control group did not change.

While the majority of studies into the impact of creative activities on physical and psychological well-being have been conducted with participants who are suffering from a mental illness of some kind, it may be that the therapeutic effects of creativity (such as absorption, engagement, greater self-esteem, enhancement of perceived control, as well as increased energy and happiness) could be equally well experienced by people who are mentally healthy. This is something that researchers need to look at in more depth.

Workaholism

1 POINT

The term "workaholic" originated in the early 1970s to describe someone for whom work has literally become an addiction. A workaholic feels compelled to work, so they stay at the office for long hours and regularly bring work home. They might also take work on holiday—perhaps not in the form of paperwork; it might be their mobile phone, PDA or laptop.

There are times when we think it's good to be busy—it can help keep your mind off worrying about the future and stop you dwelling on problems from the past. So sometimes keeping yourself occupied can pay dividends. So keeping busy can help your emotional well-being, and can simply indicate that you're a "doer," a person who can be relied on to get the task done. On the other hand, if you take on too much, any benefits of keeping busy are outweighed by the effects of overworking such as additional stress, negative mood, and increased physical illness.

Of course you don't have to be a full-blown workaholic to feel the negative effects of being constantly busy. In one study, air traffic controllers reported more health problems such as headaches and stomach pains, and more negative moods than usual on days when workload was high, or when interactions with colleagues and bosses were poor. In addition, daily increases in job stressors were also related to short-term decreases in happiness. So you do need to think carefully about what being busy means to you—are you keeping a healthy work/life balance, and staying busy but productive, or are you trying to take on too much at once?

Interestingly, workaholics don't actually enjoy being busy, so in that respect they're different from work enthusiasts. Despite working very long hours, workaholics aren't necessarily highly productive either, and in fact they may be very inefficient due to their perfectionism and inability to delegate. Workaholism, like any other addiction, can have a domino effect, not only causing problems at work, but leading to personal and social difficulties as well as health problems.

Tips to reduce your busyness

- Organize yourself—keep a notebook or a diary to jot down appointments, notes, and reminders. Set up a filing system if you haven't got one already.

- Learn how to delegate effectively.

- Ask for support from colleagues and friends.

- Learn how to say "no" to additional work assertively.

- Plan! Set goals (see entry 77) and stick to them.

- Avoid time wasters—resist the temptation to read and respond to every email as it arrives.

- Use the phone instead of email; it's quicker and easier.

- Recharge your batteries—at lunchtime get some fresh air, or visit an art gallery (see entry 50).

- Start the day by making inroads into your big projects—leave administrative tasks and chores till last.

- Don't allow your calendar to fill up with meetings—if this is a danger, ask yourself whether you can provide your input in a different way.

Vocation

☺ **2 POINTS**

How you view your job has implications for your happiness. According to psychologist Amy Wrzesniewski and colleagues, there are three distinct ways to view your job. The first is focused on doing it for the money and because you have to, not because you want to. The second is to see your job as a career, focusing on advancement, although money and benefits are also important because they act as a sign of progression. The final way is to view your job as a calling; pay and promotion are important, but the primary motivator is a sense of personal fulfillment. Research indicates that those who perceive their work as a calling experience greater satisfaction both in work and outside.

Wrzesniewski suggests that even if you have limited choice over the job you do it's still possible to craft your work so as to maximize happiness. Although some occupations seem to fall more naturally into one category or the other, you can create meaning in whatever work you do. For example, one study showed that a group of 24 education administrators were equally divided between those who perceived their work as a job, a career, and a calling.

In a study of hospital cleaners, some did only the minimum of tasks and restricted the amount of interaction they had with patients, visitors, and other staff. They disliked their job and judged it to be low-skilled. In contrast, other cleaners crafted the job to include additional tasks, as well as frequent interactions with other people. These cleaners liked their job and felt the work was highly skilled, engaging in many other tasks that helped their department run more smoothly. Clearly these two groups are doing the same job, but they give it a different meaning. As a result those who perceive the work as a calling (the second group) are far happier than the first.

Celebrity worship
2 POINTS ☹

The desire for fame has grown in the last couple of decades and this increasing incidence of obsession with famous people, whether supermodels, movie stars, or athletes, has led psychologists to create a new medical condition, called Celebrity Worship Syndrome.

There are two avenues of thought—one which suggests that this is perfectly healthy, evolutionary behavior, known more popularly as the survival of the fittest. It's to be expected because it's exactly what cavemen would have done thousands of years ago—tried to emulate the people who had higher status in order to ensure our own survival. The other perspective is that this Celebrity Worship Syndrome is an entirely unhealthy condition whereby, because people have trouble forming lasting, trusting relationships with ordinary people, they prefer to live out their own lives through the lives of their chosen celebrity.

Which is it to be? Harmless fun or obsession? Until there is further practical research carried out we won't know for sure. But in the meantime, other studies suggest that even "low level" celebrity worship reflects poorer psychological well-being, in terms of greater anxiety and depression. So if you find that you're spending more and more time following the lives of your favorite pop-stars or actors, then it's probably time to take a take a step back and consider using your time in a way which is more likely to make you happy (see entry 46).

Having children

☺ **3 POINTS**

We often assume that children bring a great deal of happiness and contentment to parent's lives: ask any of your friends, family, or colleagues who have children what is the greatest source of joy in their lives and chances are they'll say "my kids." Research has shown that for both married and single mothers, having a child is associated with increased well-being and happiness. Further research suggests, however, that the overall picture is not quite as clear cut as that; having children affects your life in very different ways depending on whether you're male or female, married, single, or cohabiting. For example, in contrast to the positive effect on married or single mothers, cohabiting, unmarried mothers experience significant declines in both their social and psychological well-being when they give birth.

At the same time, for a man, becoming a parent can be associated with small declines in feelings of well-being regardless of whether he's single, cohabiting, or married, although single fathers fare worse.

This particular research is focusing on first-time parents so it doesn't tell us what happens if they subsequently have other children, or how long these effects last. The experience of having a child and our associated feelings of well-being (or depression) may also vary depending on how much we embrace our new parenting roles. And it could be that on a daily basis, we feel quite stressed as parents, but in the long-term, most people see having children as a positive experience that adds significant meaning to their lives.

Religion

5 POINTS ☺

Religious faith also gives many people a sense of meaning and purpose in life, which can provide crucial support and help maintain well-being during difficult life events, such as bereavement and unemployment. There is growing scientific evidence that, in general, people who actively practice their religion live longer and are in general physically healthier than non-believers. This may be simply because they're less likely to smoke, drink excessively, take drugs, or engage in promiscuous sex. But are actively religious people also happier? There are a great many other benefits associated with practicing religion such as: better coping with crises; less vulnerability to depression; being more forgiving; being more hopeful and optimistic; and having more compassion.

All these positive emotions and experiences are associated with greater psychological well-being, but other explanations of the happiness of believers might be possible (see entry 70). For instance, faith communities provide social, emotional and sometimes material support, so members may feel that they belong to a like-minded community which respects and appreciates them. Even when religion isn't practiced communally, people still have a private relationship with God or another divine being which makes them feel loved and cared for, as well as giving them a source of reassurance and personal strength.

Although it's possible to be a spiritual person, that is, to be searching for self-transcendence without believing in the existence of God, spiritual and religious people have a lot in common. Spiritual people are generally happier, have better physical and psychological health, happier marriages and live longer than those who are not.

Hope

☺ # 3 POINTS

Hope is a little like optimism (see entry 30) in that it reflects a positive expectation about something happening in the future. Being hopeful is beneficial for one's psychological and physical health, by buffering against interfering, self-critical thoughts and negative emotions. On top of this, hopeful people focus more on preventing illness, for example by exercising more. And did you know that being hopeful substantially improves athletic and academic performance? This is thought to be because hopeful thinking allows you to create a mental plan which, when you focus on it, enables you to shut out interferences.

How to increase your hope

If things aren't going according to plan, it is important not to give up hope:

- Decide what your overall plan is in as much detail as you can, and what you hope to achieve by it.

- Divide your goal into smaller, more manageable sub-goals (see entry 79) so that as you achieve each sub-goal you will become more hopeful that you can achieve your overall goal.

- Motivate yourself to continue—remember what you hope to achieve and how important it is to persevere.

- Tell your family and friends about your goal—they can provide moral support if your hope starts to dwindle.

- Have a plan in mind for when things go wrong so that you can take instant action; frame any obstacles you meet as challenges to be overcome.

Volunteering

2 POINTS ☺

Formal, organized volunteering really took off in the Western world to help with reconstruction after World War I, and as a result in 1920 the first international voluntary organization was established (the Service Civil International or SCI). Since then, volunteering has been expanding to all corners of the globe.

Recently, attempts have been made to measure the contribution of volunteering to society; you might be surprised to learn from one UK study that the not-for-profit sector accounts for, on average, 5 percent of Gross Domestic Product (and in some countries exceeds 7 percent) and that volunteering specifically accounts for between 25 percent and 50 percent of this. By comparison, the utility industries account on average for only 2.3 percent of GDP and the financial services industry for 5.6 percent.

And what of the individual benefit? Why do people voluntarily give up precious time to assist other people, whether to help local school children read, protect the coral reefs in Tobago, or provide emergency relief in disaster zones? The simple fact is that volunteering, in no matter what capacity, can improve your psychological well-being, increase your life satisfaction and physical health and provide a buffer against stress. It has also been suggested that more is better: doing twice as much volunteering is roughly twice as good for you. In short, volunteering is a no-brainer.

Meditation

☺ # 5 POINTS

Meditation, the practice of focusing your attention, has been around for many thousands of years and is typically associated with Buddhism. But as we start to recognize its benefits, meditation is becoming increasingly popular in the Western world, particularly mindfulness, a technique in which you focus attention on your thoughts and actions in the present moment.

Scientific studies on meditation report a huge range of both physical and psychological benefits. Additionally, when the study participants were followed up, researchers found that these gains were maintained up to four years later. If you'd like to explore further, start by finding a local class, or a weekend beginner's retreat, in order to learn the basics from an experienced teacher, before practicing on your own. It's also important to be clear about what you want to achieve from meditating, so that you can find a suitable provider.

How meditation can increase your happiness

Studies show meditation has numerous physical and mental benefits, including:

- Enhanced resilience and ability to cope.

- Reduced stress.

- Reduced loneliness.

- Reduction in negative body image.

- Chronic pain reduction.

- Greater awareness of subtle emotions.

- Increased ability to relax.

- Greater energy and enthusiasm for life, and last but not least.

- Enhanced psychological well-being or happiness.

Matching values and actions
2 POINTS ☺

Whereas our needs (for food, shelter, and so on) are innate and evolutionary, our values are acquired; we learn them as we grow up—from our parents, friends, and society at large. Everyone needs food to survive, for example, but they learn through experience to value different types of food, whether haute cuisine or a cheeseburger. The same goes for all our other needs—they're common, but how we go about fulfilling them is what differentiates us. So your value system, or the way you prioritize your values, is unlikely to be the same as your neighbor's. The way we rank our values is what enables us to make decisions and choices every day.

Assuming that the majority of healthy adults want to be happier, the question is whether (and how) our values can help or hinder this quest. The important thing in relation to happiness is whether your actions are consistent with your values. Research suggests that people who focus on acquiring wealth and material success above other needs such as meaningful relationships, have lower satisfaction with life, and experience higher levels of depression (see entry 27). This helps to explain how stress and work/life balance have become such important topics in Western cultures in recent years—people feel they have to do things (like work longer hours) which conflict with their underlying values (such as looking after the family). What's more, studies also show that values play a vital role in whether or not experiences are remembered as happy ones. Even if an experience makes you feel very happy in the moment, you won't recall it as a happy one at a later date unless it matches your values.

Unlike needs though, values can (and do) change over your lifetime. Women who are very career-oriented in early adulthood, for example, can experience a rapid shift in values when they have children.

Finding meaning

☺ # 5 POINTS

Psychologists have shown that those people who can find meaning in the face of negative events have higher psychological well-being compared to those who can't. For example, following bereavement, people who can find meaning in their loss show better psychological as well as physical well-being a year later. Finding meaning can be done in a number of different ways. If you're religious you might attribute a loss such as the death of someone close to you as God's will. Perhaps you might acknowledge that they'd had a "good go-around," that they were no longer suffering, or even just accept the fact that sometimes things happen for no reason. You might see the death as a signal to you to lead a fuller, healthier life yourself, or as inspiration to do good works in your community. You might simply acknowledge that no one is immortal. All of these things can help you come to terms with the event. How you find your silver lining isn't that important. What matters is that it makes sense to you.

Although it's likely that the more meaningful your life is, the happier you are, the relationship between happiness and meaning in life is not that simple. For example, guerrilla revolutionaries may be unhappy with their living conditions and have low life satisfaction, but have very meaningful lives because they're fighting for a cause they strongly believe in. So the best way to explain the importance of meaning for living a happy life is to say that meaning is a prerequisite for happiness, but there are other ingredients that are also necessary.

Lifelong learning
1 POINT ☺

Rising affluence and longevity in the West, the proliferation of higher education courses, ease of access enabled by new technologies, as well as significant changes in the employment landscape have led to the emergence of something we call "lifelong learning," i.e., the requirement or aspiration to keep learning, whether in formal education or not, throughout one's life.

It's generally acknowledged that intellectual activity is as important to a long and happy life as is remaining physically fit and active. Researchers have found that continuing to learn in later life not only provides new knowledge and promotes intellectual stimulation, it increases satisfaction and gives pleasure as well. In another study of 336 learners between the ages of 50 and 71 commissioned by the UK's Department for Education and Employment in 1999, 80 percent reported a positive impact in the following areas: their enjoyment of life, their self-confidence, how they felt about themselves, satisfaction with other areas of their life, and their ability to cope with everyday life.

Other advantages of learning included improvements in their ability to stand up and be heard, and their willingness to take responsibility, broadened horizons and outlook, increased personal satisfaction, meeting people and more social interaction, and being better able to deal with other people. And on top of all these benefits, older students also reported being happier and having improved quality of life.

Conclusion

We hope this book has provided you with some insight into the origins of happiness and the everyday things which can affect it positively or negatively, as well as some practical ideas and inspiration about what you can do differently to increase your own happiness.

Some of the information may have seemed very much like common sense, while some may have seemed surprising or counter-intuitive. The main message throughout is that you don't have to leave your happiness up to chance; there are many thing you can do to increase the odds of being psychologically fitter, such as investing time and energy into building relationships, acknowledging the reality behind money, fame, and materialism, and being open to trying new things. As we get older, many of us stick with old habits, some of which can be unhelpful; now you have some new ideas about the little things you can do which will make a difference.

Hopefully you now understand that becoming happier actually involves some consistent effort on your part—and that while your genes may have given you a head start in the happiness stakes, you shouldn't necessarily expect to be happier no matter what happens to you in life. Today's world can be complex and stressful for many people, whatever your age or gender, and regardless of whether you work or not. Now that you have the background knowledge, you can put some of the suggestions into practice and see what works best for you.

It's important to acknowledge that no one can be happy all the time. Everyone will experience some sadness, disappointment, or other negative emotion at some point in their lives, this is part of what it means to be human, and without negative emotions, you wouldn't be able to appreciate positive emotions. In fact, there are some negative emotions which can lead to positive outcomes, by propelling you into action.

Finally, you can do a lot yourself to explore new (and old!) ways of being happy. This a very topical subject—after all, most of us would like to be happier—so you'll be able to find a great deal of information about it on the internet and in bookstores. Do be aware, however, that some will make unsubstantiated claims. There are plenty of very accessible websites, books, and blogs which are based on science, and which will add depth and color to *The Happiness Equation*, so don't be afraid to explore them. Just use your common sense in deciding which are reliable, or right for you.

So, having read this book, what's stopping you? Go out and live your life to its happiest.

Resources

CHAPTER 1

1. Age

Mroczek, D. K.& Kolarz, C.M (1998). The effect of age on positive and negative affect: A developmental perspective on happiness. *Journal of Personality and Social Psychology*, 75(5), 1333-1349.

Lacey, H.P., Smith, D.M. & Ubel, P.A. (2006). Hope I die before I get old: Mispredicting happiness across the adult lifespan. *Journal of Happiness Studies*, 7(2), 167-182

Staudinger, U.M., Bluck, S. & Herzberg, P.Y. (2003). Looking back and looking ahead: Adult age differences in consistency of diachronous ratings of subjective well-being. *Psychology and Aging*, 18(1), 13-24.

2. Gender

Fujita, F., Diener, E. & Sandvik, E. (1991). Gender differences in negative affect and well-being: The case for emotional intensity. *Journal of Personality and Social Psychology*, 61(3), 427-434.

Myers, D. (2000).The funds, friends and faith of happy people. *American Psychologist*, 55(1), 56-67

3. Money

Diener, E. & Oishi, S. (2000). Money and happiness: Income and subjective well-being across nations. In E. Diener & E.M. Suh (185-218). *Culture and subjective well-being*. Cambridge, MA, US: The MIT Press.

Myers, D. G., & Diener, E. (1996). The pursuit of happiness. *Scientific American*, 274, 54–56.

4. Feeling healthy

Diener, E., Suh, E.M. Lucas, R.E. (1999) Subjective well-being: Three decades of progress. *Psychological Bulletin*, 125(2), 276-302.

Kubzansky, LD. & Thurston, R.C. (2007). Emotional vitality and incident coronary heart disease: Benefits of healthy psychological functioning. *Archives of General Psychiatry*, 64(12), 1393-1401.

Salovey, P., Rothman, A.J., Detweiler, J.B. & Steward, W.T. (2000). Emotional states and physical health. *American Psychologist*, 55(1), 110-121.

5. Nutrition

Bodnar, L.M. & Wisner, K.L (2005) Nutrition and depression: Implications for improving mental health among childbearing-aged women. *Biological Psychiatry*, 58(9), 679-685.

De Vriese, S.R. Christophe, A.B. & Maes, M., (2003) Lowered serum n-3 polyunsaturated fatty acid (PUFA) levels predict the occurrence of postpartum depression further evidence that lowered n-PUFAs are related to major depression, *Life Sciences*, 73, 3181–3187

Gesch, B. (2005). The potential of nutrition to promote physical and behavioural well-being. In: F.A Huppert, N. Baylis and B. Keverne. *The science of well-being* (pp. 171-214). New York, NY, US: Oxford University Press.

7. Beauty

American Society of Aesthetic Plastic Surgery http://www.surgery.org/press/news-release.php?iid=465

Diener, E., Wolsic, B. & Fujita, F. (1995). Physical attractiveness and subjective well-being. *Journal of Personality and Social Psychology*, 69(1), 120-129.

Kent, G. (2002). Testing a model of disfigurement: Effects of a skin camouflage service on well-being and appearance anxiety. *Psychology & Health*, 17(3), 377-386.

Martin, K.A., Leary, M.R. & Rejeski, W. J. (2000). Self-presentational concerns in older adults: Implications for health and well-being. *Basic and Applied Social Psychology*, 22(3), 169-179

8. Mental Well-Being

WHO depression statistics: http://www.who.int/mental_health/management/depression/definition/en/accessed 31/01/08

Jahoda, M. (1958). *Current concepts of positive mental health*. New York, NY, US, Basic Books.

9. Extrovert Personality

Costa, P.T. & McCrae, R.R. (1980). Influence of extraversion and neuroticism on subjective well-being: Happy and unhappy people. *Journal of Personality and Social Psychology*,38(4), 668-678.

DeNeve, K. M., & Cooper, H. (1998). The happy personality: A meta-analysis of 137 personality traits and subjective well-being. Psychological Bulletin, 124, 197–229.

Steel, P., Schmidt, J. & Shultz, J. (2008). Refining the relationship between personality and subjective well-being. *Psychological Bulletin*, 134(1), 138-161.

10. Social Class

Lachman, M.E. & Weaver, S.L. (1998).The sense of control as a moderator of social class differences in health and well-being. Journal of Personality and Social Psychology, 74(3), 763-773.

Myers, D.G. & Diener, E. (1995). Who is happy? *Psychological Science*, 6(1), 10-19.

Nettle, D. (2005). *Happiness. The science behind your smile*. New York. Oxford University Press.

11. Sunshine

Epperson, C.N. ,Terman, M., Terman, J.S., Hanusa, B.H., Oren, D.A., Peindl, K.S. & Wisner, K.L. (2004). Randomized clinical trial of bright light therapy for antepartum depression: preliminary findings, *Journal of Clinical Psychiatry* 65, 421–425.

Grant, W.B & Holick, M.F. (2005). Benefits and requirements of vitamin D for optimal health: A review. *Alternative Medicine Review* 10 (2), 94 – 111.

12. Community spirit

Helliwell, J. F.; Putnam, R. D. (2005). The social context of well-being. In: F.A. Huppert, N. Baylis, B. Keverne (Eds.) (435-459). *The science of well-being*. New York, NY, US: Oxford University Press.
http://www.worldvaluessurvey.org/

13. Poverty

Biswas Diener, R. & Diener, E. (2001). Making the best of a bad situation: Satisfaction in the slums of Calcutta. *Social Indicators Research*, 55(3), 329-352.

Diener, E & Diener, C. (1996). Most people are happy. *Psychological Science*,7(3), 181-185.

Average salaries – United Nations Statistics:
http://unstats.un.org/unsd/demographic/products/socind/inc-eco.htm Retrieved 11th Feb 2008.

14. Luck

Day, L. & Maltby, J. (2003). Belief in good luck and psychological well-being: The mediating role of optimism and irrational beliefs. *Journal of Psychology: Interdisciplinary and Applied*, 137(1), 99-110.

Wiseman, R. (2004). *The Luck Factor*. London. Arrow Books.

15. Post-traumatic growth

Baumeister, R. F. & Vohs, K D. (2002).The pursuit of meaningfulness in life. In C.R. Snyder and S.J. Lopez (Eds.). *Handbook of positive psychology*. (pp. 608-618). New York, NY, US: Oxford University Press.

Frankl, V.E. (1963). *Man's search for meaning*. New York, Simon and Schuster.

Tennen, H. & Affleck, G. (2002). The pursuit of meaningfulness in life. In C.R. Snyder and S.J. Lopez (Eds.). *Handbook of positive psychology* (pp. 584-597). New York, US: Oxford University Press.

16. Political oppression

Inglehart, R. & Klingemann, H.D. (2000). Genes, culture, democracy, and happiness. In E. Diener & E.M.Suh. (165-183). *Culture and subjective well-being*. Cambridge, MA, US: The MIT Press.

Veenhoven, R. (2000). Freedom and happiness: A comparative study in forty-four nations in the early 1990s. In E. Diener & E.M.Suh. (257-288). *Culture and subjective well-being*. Cambridge, MA, US: The MIT Press.

17. Collectivist Culture

Diener, E., Oishi, S. & Lucas, R.E. (2003). Personality, culture, and subjective well-being: Emotional and cognitive evaluations of life. *Annual Review of Psychology*, 54, 403-425.

Kitayama, S., Markus, H. R. & Kurokawa, M (2000). Culture, emotion, and well-being: Good feelings in Japan and the United States. *Cognition & Emotion*, 14(1), 93-124.

Oishi, S. , Diener, E. & Choi, D. (2007). The dynamics of daily events and well-being across cultures: When less is more. *Journal of Personality and Social Psychology*, 93(4), 685-698.

18. Contact with nature

Burns, G.W. (2005). Naturally happy, naturally healthy: the role of the natural environment in well-being. In: F.A.Huppert, N. Baylis and B. Keverne (Eds.) The *science of well-being*. (pp. 405-431) New York, NY, US: Oxford University Press.

Dasgupta, P. (2001). *Human well-being and the natural environment*. New York, NY, US: Oxford University Press.

Hartig, T., Evans, G. W., Jamner, L. D., Davis, D. S., & Gärling, T. (2003). Tracking restoration in natural and urban field settings. *Journal of Environmental Psychology*, 23, 109–123.

19. Adaptation

Brickman, P., Coates, D. & Janoff-Bulman, R. (1978). Lottery winners and accident victims: Is happiness relative? *Journal of Personality and Social Psychology*, 36(8), 917-927.

Gardner, J. & Oswald, A.J. (2007) Money and mental wellbeing: A longitudinal study of medium-sized lottery wins, *Journal of Health Economics*, 26, 49-60.

CHAPTER 2
20. Negative Emotions

Carver, C S., & Scheier, M. F. (1990). Origins and functions of positive and negative affect: A control-process view. *Psychological Review*, 97, 19-35.

Fredrickson, B. L. (2001). The role of positive emotions in positive psychology: The broaden-and-build theory of positive emotions. *American Psychologist*, 56, 218-226.

21. Feeling good

Fredrickson, B.L. (2001). The role of positive emotions in positive psychology: The broaden-and-build theory of positive emotions.

American Psychologist, 56(3), 218-226.
Fredrickson, B.L., Tugade, M. M. & Waugh, C.E. (2003). What good are positive emotions in crisis? A prospective study of resilience and emotions following the terrorist attacks on the United States on September 11th, 2001. *Journal of Personality and Social Psychology*, 84(2), 365-376.

22. Lack of Confidence
Bandura, A. (1997). *Self-efficacy: The exercise of control*. New York: Freeman.
Maddux, J.R. (2002). Self-efficacy: The power of believing you can. In C.R. Snyder, & S.J. Lopez, (Eds.), *Handbook of positive psychology* (pp.277-287). New York: Oxford University Press.
Pajares (2002). Overview of social cognitive theory and of self-efficacy. Retrieved March 21 2008 at ttp://www.des.emory.edu/mf

23. Powerlessness
Haidt, J. & Rodin, J. (1999). Control and efficacy as interdisciplinary bridges. *Review of General Psychology*, 3(4), 317-337.
Langer, J. & Rodin, E.J. (1977). Long-term effects of a control-relevant intervention with the institutionalized aged. *Journal of Personality and Social Psychology*, 35(12), 897-902.

24. Vitality
Kasser, V. G. & Ryan, R.M. (1999). The relation of psychological needs for autonomy and relatedness to vitality, well-being and mortality in a nursing home. *Journal of Applied Social Psychology*, 29(5), 935-954.
Ryan, RM. & Frederick, C. (1997). On energy, personality, and health: Subjective vitality as a dynamic reflection of well-being. *Journal of Personality*, 65(3), 529-565.

25. Positive Illusions
Brookings, J. B. & Serratelli, A.J. (2006). Positive Illusions: Positively Correlated with Subjective Well-Being, Negatively Correlated with a Measure of Personal Growth. *Psychological Reports*, 98(2).
Taylor, S.E. (1989). *Positive illusions: Creative self-deception and the healthy mind*. New York, NY, US: Basic Books.

26. Curiosity
Kashdan, T.B. & Roberts, J.E. (2006). Affective outcomes in superficial and intimate interactions: Roles of social anxiety and curiosity. *Journal of Research in Personality*, 40(2), 140-167.
Park, N., Peterson, C. & Seligman, M.E.P. (2004). Strengths of character and well-being. *Journal of Social & Clinical Psychology*, 23(5), 603-619.

27. Depression
World Health Organization website accessed 21st March 2008: http://www.searo.who.int/en/section1174/section1199/section1567_6741.htm
Caspi, A., Sugden, K., Moffitt, T.E., Taylor, A., Harrington, H. ,

McClay, J., Mill, J., Martin, J., Braithwaite, A. & Poulton, R. (2003). Influence of life stress on depression: Moderation by a polymorphism in the 5-HTT gene. *Science*, 301(5631), 386-389.
Cited in S. Lyubomirsky. (2007.) *The how of happiness; a practical approach to getting the life you want*. Great Britain. Sphere.

28. Humility
Collins, J. (2001). *Good to Great: Why some companies make the leap…and others don't*. London. Random House.
King, L.A & Hicks, J.A (2007). Whatever happened to 'What might have been'? Regrets, happiness, and maturity. *American Psychologist*, 62(7), 625-636.

29. Pessimism
Diener, E. (2003). What Is Positive About Positive Psychology: The Curmudgeon and Pollyanna. *Psychological Inquiry*, 14(2) 115-120.
Norem, J. K. & Chang, E. C. (2002). The positive psychology of negative thinking. *Journal of Clinical Psychology*, 58(9) 993-1001.
Norem, J.K. & Illingworth, K. S. S. (2004). Mood and performance among defensive pessimists and strategic optimists. *Journal of Research in Personality*, 38(4), 351-366

30. Optimism
Brisette, I., Scheier, M.F. & Carver, C.S. (2002). The role of optimism in social network development, coping and psychological adjustment during a life transition. *Journal of Personality and Social Psychology*, 82, 101-111.
Carver, C.S. & Scheier, M. F. (2002). Optimism. In C.R. Snyder & S.J. Lopez (Eds.) *Handbook of positive psychology*. (pp. 231-243). New York, NY, US: Oxford University Press.
Seligman, M.E.P. (1991). Learned Optimism. New York: Knopf.

31. Resilience
Fredrickson, B.L., Tugade, M.M., Waugh, C.E. & Larkin, G.R. (2003). What good are positive emotions in crisis? A prospective study of resilience and emotions following the terrorist attacks on the United States on September 11th, 2001. *Journal of Personality and Social Psychology*, 84(2), 365-376.
Linley, P.A., & Joseph, S. (2004). Positive changes following trauma and adversity: a review. *Journal of Traumatic Stress Studies*, 17, 11-21.

32. Acceptance
Hayes, S.C., Strosahl, K.D. & Wilson, K.G. (1999). *Acceptance and commitment therapy: An experiential approach to behavior change*. New York, NY, US: Guilford Press.
McCracken, L.M. & Eccleston, C. (2003). Coping or acceptance: what to do about chronic pain? *Pain* 105, 197–204.
Van Damme, S., Crombez, G., Van Houdenhove, B., Mariman, A. & Michielsen, W.R (2006). Well-being in patients with chronic fatigue syndrome: The role of acceptance. *Journal of Psychosomatic Research*, 61(5), 595-599.

33. Stress

The Health & Safety Executive website, accessed 20th March 2008 http://www.hse.gov.uk/stress/research.htm

Herbert, J. (1997). Stress, the brain and mental illness. *British Medical Journal*, 315, 530-535

34. Poor time management

Boniwell, I. (2005). Beyond time management: How the latest research on time perspective and perceived time use can assist clients with time-related concerns. *International Journal of Evidence Based Coaching and Mentoring*, 3(2), 61-74.

Macan, T. H. (1996). Time-management training: Effects on time behaviors, attitudes and job performance. *Journal of Psychology: Interdisciplinary and Applied*, 130(3), 229-236.

35. Too much choice

Iyengar, S.S., Wells, R.E. & Schwartz, B. (2006) Doing Better but Feeling Worse: Looking for the 'Best' Job Undermines Satisfaction. *Psychological Science*, 17(2), 143-150

Schwartz, B. (2000) Self-determination: The tyranny of freedom. *American Psychologist*, 55(1), 79-88

36. Gratitude

Emmons, R. A. & McCullough, M.E. (2003). Counting blessings versus burdens: An experimental investigation of gratitude and subjective well-being in daily life. *Journal of Personality and Social Psychology*, 84(2), 377-389.

Emmons, R.A. & Crumpler, C.A. (2000). Gratitude as a human strength: Appraising the evidence. *Journal of Social & Clinical Psychology*, 19(1), Special issue: Classical Sources of Human Strength: A Psychological Analysis 56-69

37. Unhappy Endings

Fredrickson, B. (2000). Extracting meaning from past affective experiences: The importance of peaks, ends, and specific emotions. *Cognition & Emotion*, 14(4), 577-606

38. Forgiving others

McCullough, M.E. & Witvliet, C.V. (2002). The psychology of forgiveness. In: Snyder, C. R.; Lopez, Shane J. (Eds.) *Handbook of positive psychology* (pp 446-458). New York, NY, US: Oxford University Press.

Witvliet, C. V, Ludwig, T.E. & Vander Laan, K L. (2001). Granting forgiveness or harboring grudges: Implications for emotion, physiology and health. *Psychological Science*, 12(2), 117-123.

39. Coping well

Niederhoffer, K.G.& Pennebaker, J.W. (2002). Sharing one's story: On the benefits of writing or talking about emotional experience. In: C.R. Snyder & S.J. Lopez, (Eds.) *Handbook of positive psychology*. (pp. 573-583). New York, NY, US: Oxford University Press.

Zeidner, M.& Endler, N.S. (1996). *Handbook of coping: Theory,*

research, applications. Oxford, England: John Wiley & Sons.

40. Fixed mindset

Dweck, C.S. (2006). *Mindset: The new psychology of success*. New York, NY, US: Random House.

41. Worrying

Nolen-Hoeksema.S. (2003). *Women who think too much*. New York. Henry Holt.

42. Positive time perceptions

Boniwell, I. & Zimbardo, P.G. (2004). Balancing time perspective in pursuit of optimal functioning. In P.A. Linley & S. Joseph (Eds.), *Positive Psychology in Practice*. New Jersey: Wiley.

43. Comparing yourself

Lyubomirsky, S & Ross, L. (1997). Hedonic consequences of social comparison: A contrast of happy and unhappy people. *Journal of Personality and Social Psychology* 73(6), 1141-1157.

CHAPETR 3
44. Finding the flow

Csikszentmihalyi, M. (2002). *Flow*. London, Rider.

45. Lack of exercise

Herman, S , Blumenthal, J.A, & Babyak, M. (2002). Exercise therapy for depression in middle-aged and older adults: Predictors of early dropout and treatment failure. *Health Psychology*, 21(6), 553-563.

46. Watching TV

Bruni, L. & Stanca, L. (2006). Income aspirations, television and happiness: Evidence from the world values survey, *Kyklos*, 59 (2), 209–225.

Frey, B.S., Benesch, C. & Stutzer, A (2007). Does watching TV make us happy? *Journal of Economic Psychology*, 28(3), 283-313.

Layard, R. (2005). *Happiness: Lessons from a new science*. New York, Penguin.

47. Dancing

Kim, S. & Kim, J.(2007). Mood after various brief exercise and sport modes: Aerobics, hip-hop dancing, ice skating, and body conditioning. *Perceptual and Motor Skills*, 104(3, Pt2), 1265-1270.

Atterbury, C., Sorg, J. & Larson, M.A. (1983). Aerobic dancing in a long-term care facility. *Physical & Occupational Therapy in Geriatrics*, 2(3), 71-73.

48. Gardening

Gigliotti, C.M. & Jarrott, S.E. (2005). Effects of Horticulture Therapy on Engagement and Affect. *Canadian Journal on Aging*, 24(4), 367-377.

Heliker, D., Chadwick, A. & O'Connell, T. (2000). The meaning of gardening and the effects on perceived well being of a gardening project on diverse populations of elders. *Activities, Adaptation & Aging*, 24(3), 35-56.

49. Having a hobby
Dik, B.J. & Hansen, J.C. (2008). Following passionate interests to well-being. *Journal of Career Assessment*, 16(1), 86-100.
France: time use statistics.
http://www.insee.fr/en/ffc/chifcle_fiche.asp?tab_id=459 Accessed 7th March 2008.
UK time use statisics: http://www.statistics.gov.uk/articles/no-journal/time_use_2005.pdf Accessed 7th March 2008

50. Visiting an art gallery
Clow, A. & Fredhoi, C., (2006) Normalisation of salivary cortisol levels and self-report stress by a brief lunch-time visit to an art gallery by London City workers. *Journal of holistic healthcare*. 3 (2).

51. Making music
Hills, P. & Argyle, M. (1998). Musical and religious experiences and their relationship to happiness. *Personality and Individual Differences*,. 25(1), 91-102.

52. Playing
Gill, T. (2008) Space-oriented children's policy: Creating child-friendly communities to improve children's well-being. *Children & Society* 22 (2), 136–142
Pellegrini, A.D., Dupuis, D. & Peter K. (2007). Play in evolution and development. *Developmental Review*, 27(2), 261-276.

53. Binge drinking
Adams, R.E., Boscarino, J.A. & Galea, S. (2006). Alcohol use, mental health status and psychological well-being 2 years after the World Trade Center attacks in New York City. *American Journal of Drug and Alcohol Abuse*, 32(2), 203-224.
Graham, K., Massak, A. & Demers, A. (2007). Does the association between alcohol consumption and depression depend on how they are measured? *Alcoholism: Clinical and Experimental Research*, 31(1), 78-88

54. Smiling
Neuhoff, C.C. & Schaefer, C. (2002). Effects of laughing, smiling, and howling on mood. *Psychological Reports*, 91(3), 1079-1080.
Soussignan, R. (2002). Duchenne smile, emotional experience, and autonomic reactivity: A test of the facial feedback hypothesis. *Emotion*, 2(1), 52-74.

55. Insomnia
Hamilton, N. A., Gallagher, M.W. & Preacher, K. J.(2007) Insomnia and well-being, *Journal of Consulting and Clinical Psychology*, 75(6), 939-946.

Hamilton, N. A., Nelson, C., Stevens, N. & Kitzman, H. (2007). Sleep and psychological well-being. *Social Indicators Research*, 82, 147–163.

56. Keeping a diary
Pennebaker, J.W. & Beall, S.K (1986). Confronting a traumatic event: Toward an understanding of inhibition and disease. *Journal of Abnormal Psychology*, 95(3), 274-281.
Sheffield, D., Duncan, E. & Thomson, K. (2002). Written emotional expression and well-being: Result from a home-based study. *Australasian Journal of Disaster and Trauma Studies*, 6(1)

57. Savouring
Bryant, F.B. & Veroff, J.(2007). *Savoring: A new model of positive experience* .Mahwah, NJ, US: Lawrence Erlbaum Associates Publishers.
Wood, J. V., Heimpel, S. A., & Michela, J. L. (2003). Savoring versus dampening: Self-esteem differences in regulating positive affect. *Journal of Personality and Social Psychology*, 85, 566–580.

58. Laughter
Martin, R.A. (2001). Humor, laughter, and physical health: Methodological issues and research findings. *Psychological Bulletin*, Vol 127(4), 504-519.
Skevington, S.M.& White, A.(1998) Is laughter the best medicine? *Psychology & Health*, 13(1), 157-169.

59. Recreational drugs
Degenhardt, L., Hall, W. & Lynskey, M. (2001). Alcohol, cannabis and tobacco use among Australians: A comparison of their associations with other drug use and use disorders, affective and anxiety disorders, and psychosis. *Addiction*, 96(11), 1603-1614.

CHAPTER 4:
60. Love
Baumeister, R.F. & Leary, M.R. (1995). The need to belong: Desire for interpersonal attachments as a fundamental human motivation. *Psychological Bulletin*, 117(3), 497-529.
Hendrick, S. & Hendrick, C. (2002) Love. In: Snyder, C. R.; Lopez, Shane J. (Eds) *Handbook of positive psychology*. New York, NY, US: Oxford University Press, pp 472-484.

61. Widowhood
Bonanno, G. A. (2004). Loss, trauma, and human resilience: have we underestimated the human capacity to thrive after extremely aversive events? *American Psychologist*, 59(1), 20-28.
Lucas, R.E., Clark, A.E. & Georgellis, Y. (2003). Reexamining adaptation and the set point model of happiness: Reactions to changes in marital status. *Journal of Personality and Social Psychology*, 84(3), 527-539.

62. Good sex

Costa, R. M., Brody, S. (2007). Women's relationship quality is associated with specifically penile - vaginal intercourse orgasm and frequency. *Journal of Sex and Marital Therapy*, Vol. 21, 319 - 327.

Lewis, V.G., Borders, D. L. (1995). Life satisfaction of single middle-aged professional women. *Journal of Counselling and Development*, Vol. 74, 93 - 100.

Smith, V. (2007). In pursuit of good sex: Self determination and the sexual experience. *Journal of Social and Personal Relationships*, Vol.24, 69 - 85.

63. Successful marriage

Nettle, D. (2006). *Happiness: the science behind your smile*. Oxford. Oxford University Press.

Harker, L. & Keltner, D. (2001). Expressions of positive emotion in women's college yearbook pictures and their relationship to personality and life outcomes across adulthood. *Journal of Personality and Social Psychology*, 80, 112-124.,

64. Cohabiting

http://www.census.gov/prod/2003pubs/censr-5.pdf US Census Bureau website retrieved 5th April 2008

Kline, G. H., Stanley, S.M., Markman, H. J., Olmos-Gallo, P.A., St. Peters, M., Whitton, S.W. & Prado, L.M. (2004). Timing Is Everything: Pre-Engagement Cohabitation and Increased Risk for Poor Marital Outcomes. *Journal of Family Psychology*, 18(2), 311-318.

65. Divorce

Coombs, R.H. (1991). Marital status and personal well-being: A literature review. *Family Relations*, 40(1), 97-102.

Hawkins, D.N. & Booth, A. (2005). Unhappily Ever After: Effects of Long-Term, Low-Quality Marriages on Well-Being. *Social Forces*, 84(1), 451-471.

Richards, M., Hardy, R. & Wadsworth, M. (1997). The effects of divorce and separation on mental health in a national UK birth cohort. *Psychological Medicine*, 27(5), 1121-1128.

66. Being Single

Myers, D.G (2000). The funds, friends and faith of happy people. *American Psychologist*, 55(1),56-67.

67 Unhappily married

Gottman, J. M. (1998). Psychology and the study of marital processes. *Annual Review of Psychology*, 49, 169–197.

Myers, D.G (2000). The funds, friends and faith of happy people. *American Psychologist*, 55(1),56-67

68. Close friends

Diener, E. & Seligman, M.E. P. (2002). Very happy people. *Psychological Science*, 13(1), 81-84.

Peterson, C. (2006). *A primer in positive psychology*. New York: Oxford University Press.

69. Acts of kindness

Lyubomirsky, S., Sheldon, K. M. & Schkade, D. (2005). Pursuing Happiness: The Architecture of Sustainable Change. *Review of General Psychology*, 9(2) 111-131.

Sheldon, K. M. & Lyubomirsky, S. (2004). Achieving Sustainable New Happiness: Prospects, Practices and Prescriptions. In P.A. Linley & S. Joseph (Eds.) *Positive psychology in practice*, (pp. 127-145). Hoboken, NJ, US: John Wiley & Sons Inc.

70. Going to church

Ellison, C.G. & Levin, J.S. (1998). The religion-health connection: Evidence, theory, and future directions. *Health Education & Behavior*, 25(6), 700-720.

Myers, D.G. (2000). The funds, friends and faith of happy people. *American Psychologist*, 55(1), 56-67

Strawbridge, W.J., Shema, S.J., Cohen, R.D. & Kaplan, G.A. (2001). Religious attendance increases survival by improving and maintaining good health behaviors, mental health, and social relationships. *Annals of Behavioral Medicine*, 23(1), 68-74

71. Family fights

Tucker, C.J., McHale, S.M. & Crouter, A.C. (2003). Conflict resolution: Links with adolescents' family relationships and individual well-being. *Journal of Family Issues*, 24(6), 715-736.

72. Broken home

Furstenberg, F.F. & Kiernan, K.E. (2001). Delayed parental divorce: How much do children benefit *Journal of Marriage & the Family*, 63(2), 446-457.

Jekielek, S.M. (1998). Parental conflict, marital disruption, and children's emotional well-being. *Social Forces*, 76, 905-935.

73. Owning a pet

Wells, D.L. (2007). Domestic dogs and human health: An overview. *British Journal of Health Psychology*, 12(1), 145-156.

74. Conflict at work

de Dreu, C.K. W., van Dierendonck, D. & Dijkstra, M.T. M. (2004). Conflict at Work and Individual Well-being. *International Journal of Conflict Management*, Vol 15(1), 6 26.

Dijkstra, M.T. M.; van Dierendonck, D. & Evers, A. (2005). Responding to conflict at work and individual well-being: The mediating role of flight behaviour and feelings of helplessness. *European Journal of Work and Organizational Psychology*, 14(2), 119-135.

75. Emotional Intelligence

Boniwell, I (2006) *Positive Psychology in a nutshell*. London: PWBC.

Goleman, D. (1996). *Emotional intelligence: why it can matter more than IQ*. London. Bloomsbury.

76. Sharing good news
Gable, S.L., Reis, H.T., Impett, E.A. & Asher, E.R. (2004). What Do You Do When Things Go Right? The Intrapersonal and Interpersonal Benefits of Sharing Positive Events. *Journal of Personality and Social Psychology*, 87(2), 228-245.
Langston, C. A. (1994). Capitalizing on and coping with daily-life events: Expressive responses to positive events. *Journal of Personality and Social Psychology*, 67, 1112–1125.

CHAPTER 5
77. Goals
Deci, E.L., Connell, J.P. & Ryan, R.M. (1989). Self-determination in a work organization. *Journal of Applied Psychology*,74(4), 580-590.
Langer, E.J. & Rodin, J. (1976). The effects of choice and enhanced personal responsibility for the aged: A field experiment in an institutional setting. *Journal of Personality and Social Psychology*, 34(2), 191-198.

78. Education
Diener, E., Suh, E.M., Lucas, R.E. & Smith, H.L. (1999). Subjective well-being: Three decades of progress. *Psychological Bulletin*, 125(2), 276-302.
Lawrence, J.W., Carver, C.S. & Scheier, M. F. (2002). Velocity toward goal attainment in immediate experience as a determinant of affect. *Journal of Applied Social Psychology*, Vol 32(4), 788-802.

79. Getting things done
Koestner, R. (2008). Reaching one's personal goals: A motivational perspective focused on autonomy. *Canadian Psychology/Psychologie canadienne*, 49(1), 60-67.
Lawrence, J. W., Carver, C.S. & Scheier, M.F. (2002). Velocity toward goal attainment in immediate experience as a determinant of affect. *Journal of Applied Social Psychology*, 32(4), 788-802.

80. Unemployment
Clark, A.E., Diener,E., Georgellis, Y. & Lucas, R. Lags and Leads in Life Satisfaction: A Test of the Baseline Hypothesis. *Economic Journal,* forthcoming. Retrieved from A Clark website: http://ftp.iza.org/dp2406.pdf 11/4/08.
Lucas, R., Clark, A., Georgellis, Y. & Diener, E. (2004). Unemployment Alters the Set-Point for Life Satisfaction. *Psychological Science*, 15, 8-13.

81. Self-esteem
Baumeister, R.F., Campbell, J.D. & Krueger, J.I. (2003). Does high self-esteem cause better performance, interpersonal success, happiness or healthier lifestyles? *Psychological Science in the Public Interest*, 4(1), 1-44.
Crocker, J. & Park, L.E. (2004). The Costly Pursuit of Self-Esteem. *Psychological Bulletin*, 130(3), 392-414.

82. Lack of self-discipline
Baumeister, R.F., Gailliot, M. & DeWall, C. N. (2006). Self-regulation and personality: How interventions increase regulatory success, and how depletion moderates the effects of traits on behavior. *Journal of Personality*, 74(6), 1773-1801.
Baumeister, R.F. & Vohs, K.D. (2004). *Handbook of self-regulation: Research, theory and applications.* New York, NY, US: Guilford Press.

83. Materialism
Kasser, T. & Grow Kasser, V. (2001). (2001). The dreams of people high and low in materialism. *Journal of Economic Psychology*, 22(6), 693-719.
Van Boven, L. (2005). Experientialism, materialism and the pursuit of happiness. *Review of General Psychology*, 9(2), 132-142.

84. Appreciate excellence
Peterson, C. & Seligman, M. E. P. (2004). Appreciation of beauty and excellence [Awe, Wonder, Elevation]. In: C. Peterson & M.E.P. Seligman. Character strengths and virtues: A handbook and classification, (pp. 537-551). Washington, DC, US: *American Psychological Association.*
Keltner, D. & Haidt, J. (2003). Approaching awe, a moral, spiritual and aesthetic emotion. *Cognition & Emotion,* 17(2), 297-314.

85. Job satisfaction
Blanchflower, D.G. & Oswald, A.J. (1999). Well-being, insecurity and the decline of American job satisfaction. Retrieved from http://www2.warwick.ac.uk/soc/economics/staff/faculty/oswald/blanchflower.pdf website 12/4/08

86. Personal growth
Bauer, J.J. & McAdams, D.P. (2004). Growth goals, maturity and well-being. *Developmental Psychology,* 40(1), 114-127.
Kwan, C.M.L, Love, G. D., Ryff, C.D. &Essex, M (2003). The role of self-enhancing evaluations in a successful life transition. *Psychology and Aging*, 18(1), 3-12.

87. Job Insecurity
Blanchflower, D.G. & Oswald, A.J. (1999). Well-being, insecurity and the decline of American job satisfaction. Retrieved from website 12/4/08: http://www2.warwick.ac.uk/fac/soc/economics/staff/faculty/oswald/blanchflower.pdf
Rocha, C., Crowell, J.H. & McCarter, A.K. (2006). The effects of prolonged job insecurity on the psychological well-being of workers. *Journal of Sociology & Social Welfare*, 33(3), 9-28.

88. Using your strengths
Peterson, C. (2006). *A primer in positive psychology.* New York. Oxford University Press. (pp.137-164).

89. Creativity

Griffiths, S. (2008). The experience of creative activity as a treatment medium. *Journal of Mental Health*, 17(1), 49-63.

Henderson, P., Rosen, D. & Mascaro, N. (2007). Empirical study on the healing nature of mandalas. *Psychology of Aesthetics, Creativity, and the Arts*, 1(3), 148-154.

90. Workaholicism

Katz, S. (2000). Busy Bodies: Activity, aging, and the management of everyday life. *Journal of Aging Studies*, 14 (2), 135-152.

Spence, J.T. & Robbins, A.S. (1992). Workaholism: Definition, measurement, and preliminary results. *Journal of Personality Assessment*, 58(1), 160-178.

91. Vocation

Wrzesniewski, A. & Dutton, J. (2001). Crafting a job: Revisioning employees as active crafters of their work. *The Academy of Management Review*, 26(2), 179-201

Wrzesniewski, A, McCauley, C., Rozin, P. & Schwartz, B. (1997). Jobs, careers and callings: People's relations to their work. *Journal of Research in Personality*, 31(1), 21-33.

92. Celebrity worship

Maltby, J., McCutcheon, L.E. & Ashe, D.D. (2001). The self-reported psychological well-being of celebrity worshippers. *North American Journal of Psychology*, 3(3), 441-452.

Sheridan, L., North, A. & Maltby, J. (2007). Celebrity worship, addiction and criminality. *Psychology, Crime & Law*, 13(6), 559-571.

93. Having children

Knoester, C. & Eggebeen, D.J. (2006). The effects of the transition to parenthood and subsequent children on men's well-being and social participation. *Journal of Family Issues*, 27(11), 1532-1560.

Nomaguchi, K. M. & Milkie, M. A. (2003). Costs and rewards of children: The effects of becoming a parent on adults' lives. *Journal of Marriage and Family*, 65, 356- 374.

Woo, H & Raley, R.K. (2005) A small extension to "costs and ro wards of children: The effects of becoming a parent on adults' lives". *Journal of Marriage and Family*, 67 (1), 216-221.

94. Religion

Lyubomirsky, S. (2007): *The how of happiness. A practical guide to getting the life you want*. Great Britain. Sphere.

Strawbridge, W.J., Cohen, R.D. & Shema, S.J. & Kaplan, George A. (1997) Frequent attendance at religious services and mortality over 28 years. *American Journal of Public Health*, 87(6), 957-961.

95. Hope

Curry, L.A., Snyder, C. R. & Cook, D.L. (1997). Role of hope in academic and sport achievement *Journal of Personality and Social Psychology*, 73(6), 1257-1267.

Lopez, S.J., Snyder, C.R., Magyar-Moe, J.L., Edwards, L.M., Pedrotti, J.T., Janowski, K., Turner, J.L. Pressgrove, C. & Hackman, A. (2004). Strategies for Accentuating Hope. In. P.A. Linley & S Joseph (Eds.) *Positive psychology in practice*. (pp. 388-404).

96. Volunteering

Piliavin, J.A. (2003). Doing well by doing good: Benefits for the benefactor. In: C.M. Keyes & J Haidt (Eds.) Flourishing: Positive psychology and the life well-lived. Washington, DC, US: *American Psychological Association*, pp. 227-247.

Van Willigen, M. (2000). Differential benefits of volunteering across the life course. *Journals of Gerontology: Series B: Psychological Sciences and Social Sciences*, 55B(5), S308-S318. http://www.jhu.edu/ccss/publications/pdf/Measuring_Civil_Society.pdf accessed 15th January 2008

97. Meditation

Brown, K. W & Ryan, R. M. (2003). The benefits of being present: Mindfulness and its role in psychological well-being. *Journal of Personality and Social Psychology*, 84(4), 822-848.

Oman, D., Hedberg, J. & Thoresen, C.E. (2006). Passage meditation reduces perceived stress in health professionals: A randomized, controlled trial. *Journal of Consulting and Clinical Psychology*, 74(4), 714-719.

98. Matching values and actions

Burroughs, J.E. & Rindfleisch, A. (2002). Materialism and well-being: A conflicting values perspective. *Journal of Consumer Research*, 29(3), 348-370.

Koestner, R. (2008). Reaching one's personal goals: A motivational perspective focused on autonomy. *Canadian Psychology/Psychologie canadienne*, 49(1), 60-67.

Srivastava, A., Locke, E.A. & Bartol, K.M. (2001). Money and subjective well-being: It's not the money, it's the motives. *Journal of Personality and Social Psychology*, 80(6), 959-971.

99. Finding meaning

McGregor, I. & Little, B.R. (1998). Personal projects, happiness and meaning: On doing well and being yourself. *Journal of Personality and Social Psychology*, 74 (2), 494-512.

Ryff, C.D. (1989). Happiness is everything, or is it? Explorations on the meaning of psychological well-being. *Journal of Personality and Social Psychology*, 57(6), 1069-1081.

100. Lifelong learning

Cusack, S.A. (1995). Developing a lifelong learning program: Empowering seniors as leaders in lifelong learning. *Educational Gerontology*, 21(4), 305-320.

Withnall, A. & Thompson, V. (2002). Older people and lifelong learning: choices and experiences. Accessed from website 20 April 2008 http://www.tlrp.org/project%20sites/withnall/

Index